VMware ThinApp 4.7 Essentials

Learn how to quickly and efficiently virtualize your applications with ThinApp 4.7

Peter Björk

[PACKT] enterprise
PUBLISHING
professional expertise distilled

BIRMINGHAM - MUMBAI

VMware ThinApp 4.7 Essentials

First published: November 2012

Production Reference: 1161112

Published by Packt Publishing Ltd.
Livery Place
35 Livery Street
Birmingham B3 2PB, UK.

ISBN 978-1-84968-628-0

www.packtpub.com

Cover Image by Artie Ng (artherng@yahoo.com.au)

Credits

Author
Peter Björk

Reviewers
Aaron Black

Adam Eckerle

Acquisition Editor
Andrew Duckworth

Lead Technical Editor
Arun Nadar

Technical Editors
Jalasha D'costa

Charmaine Pereira

Copy Editors
Brandt D'Mello

Alfida Paiva

Project Coordinator
Abhishek Kori

Proofreaders
Lydia May Morris

Stephen Silk

Indexer
Rekha Nair

Graphics
Valentina D'silva

Aditi Gajjar

Production Coordinator
Nitesh Thakur

Cover Work
Nitesh Thakur

About the Author

Peter Björk has many years of ThinApp experience. He started out working with Thinstall, and continued after VMware acquired the product in 2008, renaming it ThinApp. Peter supports ThinApp in the EMEA region. As a teacher, Peter has educated many ThinApp packagers around the world. Peter lives in Sweden with his wife and two kids, a boy and a girl.

I would like to thank the people who have supported me throughout the writing of this book. First and foremost, my thanks go out to my wonderful wife, Lena. Without her help and support, this book would never have been written. I know ThinApp to a depth not many others do, but my writing skills are clearly insufficient. Luckily, Lena has the gift of words, so with her support I managed to write this book. To my two wonderful kids, Albin and Filippa, who constantly remind me of what's important in my life. I would also like to thank my reviewers, Aaron Black and Adam Eckerle. Their valuable input was important for this book. I also thank PACKT Publishing for trusting in me to write this book. It's my first book and the team: Andrew Duckworth, Abhishek Kori, and Arun Nadar really helped me through the process. I must thank Jonathan Clark for coming up with the great idea of Thinstall, and with that created what became the better part of the my career. Last but not least, my thoughts go to the family of late Ge van Geldorp. Ge was an amazing developer and without his genius coding, ThinApp would not be what it is today. Ge, you are missed every day.

About the Reviewers

Aaron Black is a senior product manager at VMware® in the End User Computing business unit. He is currently responsible for ThinApp, ThinApp Factory, and the Horizon integration with ThinApp. At VMware, he has worked in various positions in the field as a Systems Engineer, a stint in technical marketing, and now product management. His primary domain of knowledge revolves around all things that are applications related. At previous companies, he worked as a Systems Engineer with Citrix Systems, leading a technical corporate IT team at Sprint, and solutions design for a platinum reseller of VMware and Citrix products.

Adam Eckerle is a Solutions Architect at Network Storage, Inc in Indianapolis, IN, US (`networkstorageinc.com`). He has a B.S. degree in Computer Engineering from Rose-Hulman Institute of Technology and has worked in Engineering and IT for more than 10 years. His primary focus is Datacenter Virtualization around the VMware vSphere platform. Other areas of focus are EMC storage platforms, Cisco UCS x86 server virtualization, and Vblock solutions. Among Adam's industry certifications are Microsoft Certified IT Professional, VMware Certified Professional (4 & 5), and Cisco Data Center Unified Computing Design Specialist.

I'd like to thank my wife, Alexis, and our two young sons, Drew and Ethan, who have allowed me to follow my dreams and make every day worth living.

www.PacktPub.com

Support files, eBooks, discount offers and more

You might want to visit www.PacktPub.com for support files and downloads related to your book.

Did you know that Packt offers eBook versions of every book published, with PDF and ePub files available? You can upgrade to the eBook version at www.PacktPub.com and as a print book customer, you are entitled to a discount on the eBook copy. Get in touch with us at service@packtpub.com for more details.

At www.PacktPub.com, you can also read a collection of free technical articles, sign up for a range of free newsletters and receive exclusive discounts and offers on Packt books and eBooks.

http://PacktLib.PacktPub.com

Do you need instant solutions to your IT questions? PacktLib is Packt's online digital book library. Here, you can access, read and search across Packt's entire library of books.

Why Subscribe?

- Fully searchable across every book published by Packt
- Copy and paste, print and bookmark content
- On demand and accessible via web browser

Free Access for Packt account holders

If you have an account with Packt at www.PacktPub.com, you can use this to access PacktLib today and view nine entirely free books. Simply use your login credentials for immediate access.

Instant Updates on New Packt Books

Get notified! Find out when new books are published by following @PacktEnterprise on Twitter, or the *Packt Enterprise* Facebook page.

Table of Contents

Preface

VMware ThinApp 4.7 is an application virtualization solution which allows its admins to package Windows applications so that they are portable.

"VMware ThinApp 4.7 Essentials" shows you how to create and deploy ThinApp packages in order to improve the portability, manageability, and compatibility of applications by encapsulating them from the underlying operating system on which they are executed.

ThinApp eliminates application conflicts, reducing the need and cost of recoding and regression testing.

No matter if you are completely new to VMware ThinApp or an experienced ThinApp packager, this is the book for you. I've made an effort to make sure that everyone can learn something in each chapter. This book will cover everything needed to become a successful ThinApp packager. This book does not talk about the competition. I wanted this book to be technically oriented and so very little, if any, is of a non-technical nature.

What this book covers

Chapter 1, *Application Virtualization*, covers basic application virtualization concepts. It also covers important concepts like isolation modes, the sandbox, and much more.

Chapter 2, *Application Packaging*, explains the whole packaging process. It takes you through a simple packaging example, which you can easily perform yourself. Entry points and the data container are explained as well as how your packaging environment affects your packages..

Chapter 3, *Deployment of ThinApp Packages*, walks you through the different methods for deployment as it's now time to deploy the package to your end users. We cover ThinApp native methods of deployment as well as using VMware View and VMware Horizon Application Manager.

Chapter 4, Updating and Tweaking Your ThinApp Project, covers how to maintain your packages using different methods and helps you choose the appropriate method for different types of updates as after a while, all applications must be updated one way or another.

Chapter 5, How to Distribute Updates, covers how to deploy your newly created updated package. ThinApp offers many different methods, so a good portion is spent on helping you identify which methods to use for which update.

Chapter 6, Design and Implementation Considerations using ThinApp, outlines general implementation guidelines. The chapter goes through things you need to be aware of in order to successfully implement ThinApp in your environment.

Chapter 7, Troubleshooting, teaches you how to conduct efficient troubleshooting of ThinApp packages, since sometimes you may face an issue while trying to package a certain application. I have shared some tips and tricks that I've picked up from my many years of ThinApp packaging.

Appendix, References, provides you with a complete Package.ini parameter reference as well as all folder macros, and environment variables supported by ThinApp.

What you need for this book

If you want to perform the examples I use throughout this book yourself, you will need a couple of applications. You will need the following:

- VMware ThinApp

You can download a free trial of VMware ThinApp from here: http://www.vmware.com/go/trythinapp.

- VMware Workstation

You can download a free trial from: http://www.vmware.com/go/tryworkstation.

- One Microsoft Windows XP and one Windows 7 virtual machine.
- Installation media for the different applications that you want to package. I use Mozilla Firefox for most of my examples. I personally prefer the old Mozilla Firefox versions. You can download the old versions from here: https://ftp.mozilla.org/pub/mozilla.org/firefox/releases/

Who this book is for

This book is for anyone who will work with ThinApp, or is interested in learning everything there is to know about ThinApp. It doesn't matter if you've never seen ThinApp before or have been using ThinApp for many years. I guarantee that everyone will learn something by reading this book.

Conventions

In this book, you will find a number of styles of text that distinguish between different kinds of information. Here are some examples of these styles, and an explanation of their meaning.

Code words in text are shown as follows: "Some folder macros share the same name as Windows variables such as `%AppData%` pointing to the users' roaming profile."

A block of code is set as follows:

```
[BuildOptions]
OptionalAppLinks=C:\Plugins\LoadMeFirst.exe; C:\Plugins\LoadMeLast.exe
```

When we wish to draw your attention to a particular part of a code block, the relevant lines or items are set in bold:

```
[BuildOptions]
OptionalAppLinks=C:\Plugins\LoadMeFirst.exe; C:\Plugins\LoadMeLast.exe
```

Any command-line input or output is written as follows:

```
048200 00000000 00000a00    Can't load library MSVCP50.dll which is
implicitly loaded by C:\Application A\DLLIAP.dll, err=53
```

New terms and **important words** are shown in bold. Words that you see on the screen, in menus or dialog boxes for example, appear in the text like this: "Clicking the **Next** button moves you to the next screen".

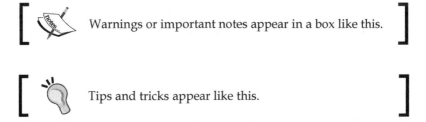

Warnings or important notes appear in a box like this.

Tips and tricks appear like this.

Reader feedback

Feedback from our readers is always welcome. Let us know what you think about this book—what you liked or may have disliked. Reader feedback is important for us to develop titles that you really get the most out of.

To send us general feedback, simply send an e-mail to `feedback@packtpub.com`, and mention the book title via the subject of your message.

If there is a topic that you have expertise in and you are interested in either writing or contributing to a book, see our author guide on www.packtpub.com/authors.

Customer support

Now that you are the proud owner of a Packt book, we have a number of things to help you to get the most from your purchase.

Errata

Although we have taken every care to ensure the accuracy of our content, mistakes do happen. If you find a mistake in one of our books—maybe a mistake in the text or the code—we would be grateful if you would report this to us. By doing so, you can save other readers from frustration and help us improve subsequent versions of this book. If you find any errata, please report them by visiting http://www.packtpub.com/support, selecting your book, clicking on the **errata submission form** link, and entering the details of your errata. Once your errata are verified, your submission will be accepted and the errata will be uploaded on our website, or added to any list of existing errata, under the Errata section of that title. Any existing errata can be viewed by selecting your title from http://www.packtpub.com/support.

Piracy

Piracy of copyright material on the Internet is an ongoing problem across all media. At Packt, we take the protection of our copyright and licenses very seriously. If you come across any illegal copies of our works, in any form, on the Internet, please provide us with the location address or website name immediately so that we can pursue a remedy.

Please contact us at copyright@packtpub.com with a link to the suspected pirated material.

We appreciate your help in protecting our authors, and our ability to bring you valuable content.

Questions

You can contact us at questions@packtpub.com if you are having a problem with any aspect of the book, and we will do our best to address it.

1
Application Virtualization

In this chapter we will cover a general overview of application virtualization and ThinApp. We will start by exploring what application virtualization is and why it is superior to local installations. We will then cover the architecture behind ThinApp and how we can manipulate and customize ThinApp packages to suit our specific requirements.

By the end of this chapter, you will have learned about:

- Application virtualization
- Why you should use application virtualization
- ThinApp architecture
- Common ThinApp vocabulary
- The sandbox
- Isolation modes
- Application linking with the help of AppLink

Application virtualization

Application virtualization encapsulates an application and all of its components into a package that is easy to deploy and manage. Using virtualization allows you to execute the application as if it was locally installed when it is not. Normally when you install an application it will register DLL files, create registry keys, and copy files into your operating system. This modifies your operating system and you will always run the risk of overwriting something already installed and breaking an existing application. By virtualizing the application, you will never install anything on the client, you will simply execute the application. There is also a virtualization layer hooking into the APIs of the application. When hooking the API for, let's say Open File, it is possible for the virtualization layer to present a virtual environment for the application, thus fooling the application into thinking it is already locally installed and therefore allowing it to execute.

The benefits of using application virtualization are many. Your operating system stays clean. By having clean machines, your clients will be more stable. A virtualized application is much easier to deploy, maintain, and retire than a natively installed one. With application virtualization, it is often possible to run two otherwise conflicting applications simultaneously on the same machine. Not using application virtualization makes it pretty much impossible to have Microsoft Office 2003 and Microsoft Office 2010 installed on the same client and run both at the same time.

ThinApp overview

VMware ThinApp is a packaging format. Like MSI and other packaging formats, ThinApp simplifies application deployment. ThinApp uses virtualization to package your application, which lets you execute the packaged application without having to install it. When using ThinApp, you simply need to have access to your package in order to use the application, as compared to the legacy MSI format in which you need to install and register your application on the local machine. As a side effect of using virtualization, you can isolate the filesystem and registry components from the locally installed applications as well as from other virtualized applications. This allows you to run conflicting applications on the same machine. Since you will never install anything locally, the use of an application will not alter your operating system. Your client will be much cleaner, more stable, and will operate faster for a longer time. ThinApp minimizes the constant reinstallation of the operating system due to repetitive application installs, which leave residue and often create conflicts that eventually leave the operating system in a degraded state necessitating a complete system rebuild.

ThinApp has one very obvious advantage over other solutions out there. It is agentless, meaning you need nothing locally installed in order to execute an application packaged with the help of ThinApp. Being agentless greatly reduces the administration overhead. When a new ThinApp version is released, you don't have to touch any existing packages already deployed. Start using the new version to capture new applications. You can happily deploy these next to an old ThinApp package since there is no conflict between ThinApp versions running side-by-side. Being agentless also lets you offer an application to a user bringing his or her own device without the need to ever touch the device. You don't run the risk of being accused of altering the user's machine.

Out of the box, ThinApp is capable of virtualizing 60 – 80 percent of your applications. Having more ThinApp knowledge and experience might allow you to virtualize up to 85 – 90 percent. You will, most of the time, never achieve 100 percent virtualization. This means you will, most of the time, have two packaging formats in place – native installation (often MSI) and ThinApp. ThinApp supports virtualizing Services, COM, and DCOM objects. ThinApp does not support virtualizing device drivers, Network visible DCOM, Global Hook DLLs, and COM+. There might be workarounds to these limitations. One of these could be to load what is not supported outside the virtual environment. One of the main reasons to virtualize an application is to keep your operating system clean. This is why ThinApp does not make many changes to the operating system when registering a ThinApp package. Registering a package will give you a certain level of shell integration, such as shortcuts, file type registrations, and a few more, but not all. Context menus are a typical example. This changed user experience might be a reason not to virtualize an application, even though ThinApp can package it. For instance, 7-Zip adds a context menu item so that when you right-click on a ZIP file in Windows Explorer, you can perform zip/unzip operations without having to open the application directly. A 7-Zip ThinApp package will happily perform zip/unzip operations when launched directly, but the users will not have access to the right-click context menu. Most of the times you can create context menus pointing to a virtualized application but it is not something ThinApp creates automatically for you when registering the package.

Even though you will probably not be able to reach 100 percent application virtualization, ThinApp adds significant value to your application's deployment and management infrastructure. Every application you manage to virtualize will be easier to maintain and cheaper to support.

ThinApp architecture

Since it cannot be mentioned too many times, ThinApp is agentless. Nothing needs to be installed on the client in order to run and use a ThinApped application. The ThinApp runtime is built into each one of the ThinApp packages you create. ThinApp does not create conflicts between different versions of ThinApp runtimes, so you can run packages built using different ThinApp versions on one single machine.

The ThinApp runtime manages file and registry access within the virtual environment. With the help of isolation modes you can decide what may or may not be modified on the native operating system. The ThinApp runtime loads processes and manages memory. Because it is the ThinApp runtime that launches a process, the runtime now monitors all API calls made by the process. The runtime is also able to intercept the API calls and manipulate both the request and reply. This is referred to as **hooking the API calls**. The ThinApp runtime hooks hundreds of Win32 APIs in order to create the virtual environment. Let's say an application tries to open a file. The ThinApp runtime sees this request, hooks it, and is now capable of passing a virtualized file to the application, instead of serving the native file to the application. The ThinApp runtime does not hook all possible Windows APIs, only the ones needed to present a virtual environment to the application package. API calls to hardware such as graphical drivers are not hooked.

A ThinApp package contains not only the ThinApp runtime, but also includes a virtualized registry and filesystem. You as a packager decide the content of the virtual environment during packaging. The virtual environment built into the package is called the read-only version of the virtual environment. The end user cannot modify the content within the package. Only you as a packager can change the content.

Changes made by either the user or the application itself are often stored in the sandbox. The sandbox content is a part of the whole virtual environment known to the application.

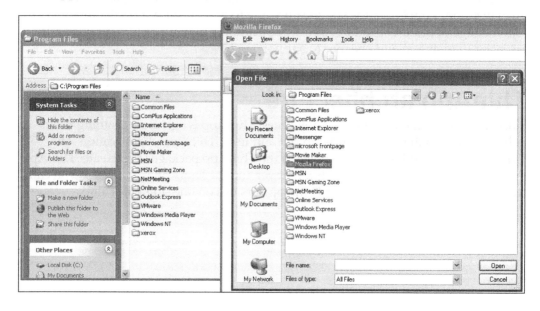

The view of the environment of a package is a merge between the physical and the virtualized. In the previous screenshot, Mozilla Firefox sees the content of native `C:\Program Files` as well as the virtualized folder called **Mozilla Firefox**. The **Mozilla Firefox** folder is not available to the operating system (Explorer window).

When the virtualized application is launched, the virtual environment is initiated by the ThinApp runtime and presented to the executing process. The application believes it is locally installed on the machine. The packaging process of ThinApp does not alter the application's files in any way. The ThinApp runtime loads the processes and by launching it, the ThinApp runtime can hook into the API calls made by the processes and present the virtual environment.

Common ThinApp vocabulary

In order to have a meaningful discussion about ThinApp, we need to agree on some common vocabulary. I prefer to give you this vocabulary earlier in the book rather than later. If you have already used ThinApp, most of this will already be known. If you are new to ThinApp, don't worry, as we will cover all of it in more detail as the book progresses.

The capturing process

This is the whole process of capturing an application. You can run **Setup Capture**, install your application, and save the capture into a project folder. The capture process analyzes all changes made to your capture machine and stores those into a project folder. These changes are what will become the virtual environment and make the captured application believe it is locally installed on the target machine.

The capture machine

This is the machine on which you run the capture process. Most of the time it's a virtual machine since that allows easy reversion to different machine states (snapshots). After successfully capturing an application, you will revert to a clean state before you capture a new application.

The project folder

This is the outcome of your capturing process. Now the real work as a packager begins. It's the project folder that contains the virtualized environment such as files and registry keys recorded during your capturing process.

The package

When you compile your project folder, the outcome will be the package. The package is what your users consume in order to execute the captured application. The package will normally be found in the `bin` folder within your project folder. A package can be one single file or multiple files, one being the data container and others being entry points.

The data container

The data container is the file containing your compiled project folder. It's the container for the whole virtual environment and the ThinApp runtime.

The entry point

Entry points are the doorways for the user to access the virtualized application. An entry point specifies what will be executed in the virtualized environment of your data container. The target of your entry point may or may not be virtualized. It is possible to have an entry point for a Java Runtime package launching your locally installed Internet Explorer. Internet Explorer would see the virtualized environment and therefore use the version of Java packaged. An entry point can also be a data container. Otherwise, if it's only an entry point, the data container must be located in the same folder as the entry point. An entry point can be used to any data container. The entry point simply searches for the specified data container's name and will happily use any data container. An entry point contains registration information such as icon, file types, object types, protocols and where to create shortcuts.

Compiling or building your ThinApp package

The building process is the process of taking the content of your project folder and compiling it into a virtual environment. This process can be issued from within ThinApp's capturing tool, **Setup Capture**, or from within your project folder by launching the `build.bat` batch file. Every time you change the content of your project folder, you'll have to recompile it in order for the changes to be applied to the package.

The build machine

This is any machine you can use to compile your project. It may or may not be your capture machine. You do not have to use a certain operating system or even a clean machine in order to compile your package. Any machine should do the trick. The build machine must have access to the ThinApp utilities folder and your project folder in order to successfully compile your project.

The ThinApp utilities folder

This is the folder created during the installation of VMware ThinApp. Most of the time it's found in `C:\Program Files\VMware\VMware ThinApp`. Since ThinApp utilities are virtualized, you can move this folder to any location. I personally store the folder on a network share for easy access from all my different capture machines.

The ThinApp runtime

This package embedded runtime allows the virtual environment to be created. The ThinApp runtime loads the virtualized application's processes and DLLs. It hooks Windows APIs in order to present a virtualized environment to the virtualized application.

Read-Only data

This is the virtual environment, filesystem, and registry, compiled into the ThinApp package. Since the package is in a compiled format, no regular end user can open this file and modify its content.

Read and write data

This is what we call the data stored in the sandbox. The sandbox is where ThinApp stores changes made to the environment by the virtualized application or the end user. Deleting the sandbox will revert the package to its read-only data state.

Folder macros

These are much like system variables in a Windows operating system, but these are ThinApp-specific variables. Some folder macros share the same name as Windows variables such as `%AppData%` pointing to the users' roaming profile. But others are different, for example `%ProgramFilesDir%` represents the system variable `%ProgramFiles%`. When you use VBScripts within your packages, you must understand that there is a difference between folder macros and system variables. The use of folder macros allows package portability. When you launch a package on an English OS, your `%ProgramFilesDir%` will be `C:\Program Files`, while on a German OS it is the same folder macro pointing to `C:\Programme`. This way, the application you virtualized will find its installation folder where it expects to find it, no matter what language of OS it's running on. You can find a list of all folder macros in *References*.

The sandbox

Many applications require the ability to write or modify data on the computer's filesystem and registry. When this need arises, ThinApp writes this data to the sandbox. This process is configurable and can be controlled through isolation modes.

The sandbox will store user settings so that these are preserved between application launches. If you delete the sandbox, the package will revert to its vanilla state. How big the sandbox will become depends on two factors: isolation modes and the behavior of the application.

The sandbox is a normal folder storing complete, fully functional versions of modified files. Let's say you run a virtualized application using .ini configuration files. Changing the application's configuration would alter the .ini file, and in your sandbox you would find the new version. It's fully functional and possible to open, for example, in native Notepad. The files are stored in folder macros, representing the path to the file. Since files are stored as native files and not in a binary blob, it's easy to perform backups of your sandbox. You can do single file restores and your antivirus software can scan its content without any problems.

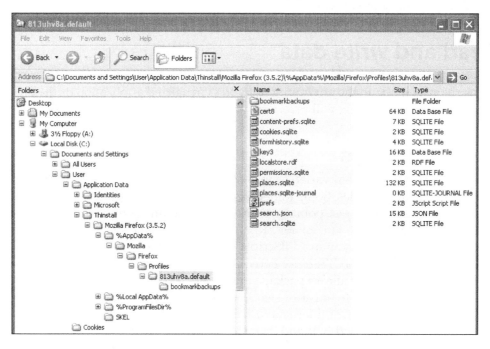

The previous screenshot shows the sandbox contents stored as plain files in a path represented by a folder macro.

Modifications to the registry are also kept in the sandbox. In order to guarantee integrity, the registry is stored in a transactional database format. This makes it a little harder to investigate the contents of the registry changes stored in the sandbox, but with the tool called `vregtool.exe` found in the ThinApp utilities folder, it's still possible. It's important to maintain the integrity of the registry since the registry in the sandbox also includes a file database, telling the ThinApp runtime where to find each file.

The registry files are found in the root of the sandbox and are all called **Registry**.

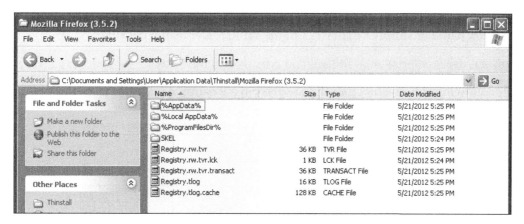

The previous screenshot is an example of sandbox contents.

The database format for storing the registry was introduced in ThinApp Version 4.0.4. With `DisableTransactionRegistry=1` in your `Package.ini` you can still use the legacy format, which uses a flat file with a backup of the last known good state. It's not very likely that you will want to use the legacy format, but in some rare implementations it has proven to speed up execution of the package, especially if the user's sandbox is stored on a network share.

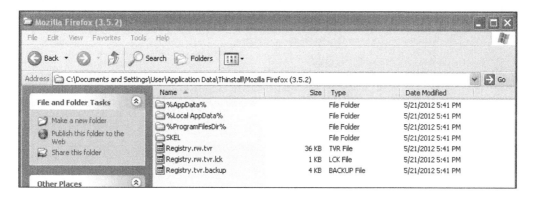

The previous screenshot is a sandbox using the legacy method of storing the registry.

The sandbox can be located anywhere as long as the end user has permission to modify the location. The sandbox will be created and updated in the context of the user.

You can specify the location of the sandbox using the parameter SandboxPath= in Package.ini (more information about Package.ini can be found in the next chapter). If you do not specify SandboxPath=, the default location will be the user's roaming profile, in a folder called Thinstall. You can override the sandbox location using environment variables or by creating a folder called either the project's sandbox name or simply Thinstall in the same folder as the package.

You can use SandboxPath= in Package.ini in different ways.

The following is how you store the sandbox in a location next to the package:

```
[BuildOptions]
SandboxPath=.
```

This is shown in the following screenshot:

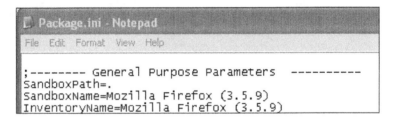

The following screenshot shows the result:

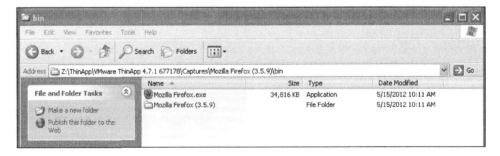

More examples are given as follows:

```
[BuildOptions]
SandboxPath=C:\Sandboxes
```

The following screenshot shows the result:

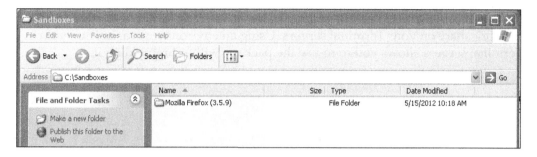

```
[BuildOptions]
SandboxPath=\\cnb\Sandboxes
```

The following screenshot shows the result:

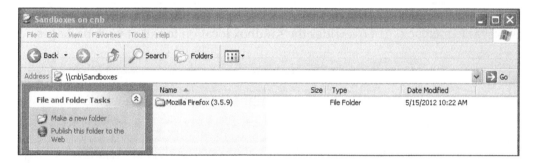

Creating a folder called **Thinstall** next to the package will change the sandbox location. This comes in handy especially during troubleshooting. By using a **Thinstall** folder, you can override the content in your existing sandbox. The **Thinstall** folder is shown in the following screenshot:

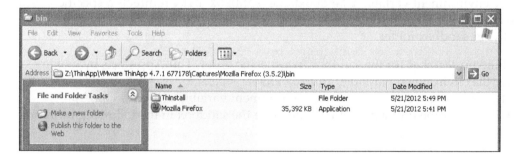

Using environment variables to override a package sandbox location allows you to use the same package in many different environments. Let's say you want to store the sandbox in the default location on laptops, while you want to store them on a network share on your Terminal servers. Using an environment variable on your Terminal servers allows you to re-use the package without rebuilding it.

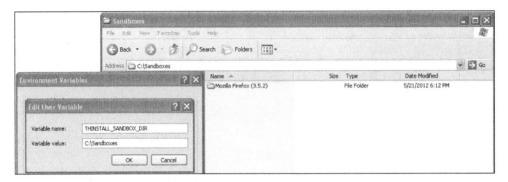

THINSTALL_SANDBOX_DIR overrides the sandbox location for all of your packages.

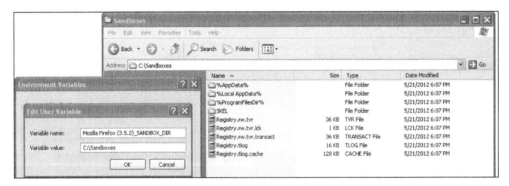

The environment variable %SandboxName_SANDBOX_DIR% redirects a specific package's sandbox location. Please note the variable value specifies the root of your sandbox folder.

ThinApp searches for the sandbox in a specific order. ThinApp starts by looking for the environment variable, %SandboxName_SANDBOX_DIR% followed by %THINSTALL_SANDBOX_DIR%. If no environment variable is found, ThinApp will look for the following folders and store the sandbox in the following locations:

- `LOCATION_OF_PACKAGE\SandboxName.ComputerName`

  For example, `C:\Program Files\Firefox\Mozilla Firefox 3.5.2.My_Computer`

- `LOCATION_OF_PACKAGE\SandboxName`

  For example, `C:\Program Files\Firefox\Mozilla Firefox 3.5`

- `LOCATION_OF_PACKAGE\Thinstall\SandboxName.ComputerName`

  For example, `C:\Program Files\Firefox\Thinstall\Mozilla Firefox 3.5.2.My_Computer`

- `LOCATION_OF_PACKAGE\Thinstall\SandboxName`

  For example, `C:\Program Files\Firefox\Thinstall\Mozilla Firefox 3.5.2`

- `SandboxPath_In_Package.ini\SandboxName.ComputerName`

  For example, `H:\Sandboxes\Mozilla Firefox 3.5.2.My_Computer`

- `SandboxPath_In_Package.ini\SandboxName`

  For example, `H:\Sandboxes\Mozilla Firefox 3.5.2`

If ThinApp fails to find `%SandboxName_SANDBOX_DIR%`, `%THINSTALL_SANDBOX_DIR%`, a `Thinstall` folder next to itself, or `SandboxPath=` in `Package.ini`, then ThinApp will create the sandbox in the default location, that is, in the user's roaming profile (`%AppData%`).

The search order for the sandbox in `%AppData%` is:

- `%AppData%\Thinstall\SandboxName.ComputerName`

  For example, `C:\Documents and Settings\User\Application Data\Thinstall\Mozilla Firefox 3.5.2.My_Computer`

- `%AppData%\Thinstall\SandboxName`

  For example, `C:\Documents and Settings\User\Application Data\Thinstall\Mozilla Firefox 3.5.2`

You can change the name of the sandbox. The default name will be taken from **Inventory name** specified during the capturing process, as shown in the following screenshot:

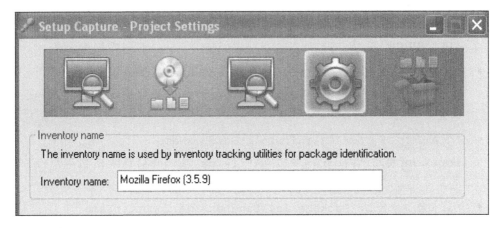

Using the parameter `SandboxName=` in `Package.ini` enables you to set the sandbox name.

Isolation modes

Isolation modes are by far the most important thing to fully understand when it comes to ThinApp. Most of the troubleshooting you will face is related to isolation modes in one way or another. Isolation modes are the packager's method of specifying what level of interaction the package is allowed to have with the underlying operating system.

You can specify different isolation modes on a per directory or registry sub-tree basis. Any child will inherit its parent isolation mode if not overridden.

ThinApp offers three different isolation modes.

Merged

Merged allows the virtualized application to interact with local files, folders, and registry keys. The package can read local elements and is able to modify local elements. Any new element will be created on the local system. If any of the virtualized elements are modified, the modifications will be stored in the sandbox.

Merged mostly mimics the behavior of a natively installed application. The actions of the package are still subject to the privileges of the user running the application. If the user is not allowed to modify a location, the standard operating system dialog box will be displayed saying so.

WriteCopy

WriteCopy will allow the package to read any local elements, but if modified, the modification will end up in the sandbox and not the local system. If you create a new file or registry key in a WriteCopy location, it will be sandboxed. Modifications made to virtualized elements will be sandboxed.

WriteCopy will protect your local system from being modified by a virtualized application. WriteCopy is often used to allow applications demanding higher privileges to be able to executed by a standard user. The application thinks it is capable of modifying `C:\Windows` but all those operations end up in the sandbox.

Full

Full isolation mode will keep the virtualized application from accessing anything locally on the underlying operating system. Physical elements are hidden from the virtualized application. If you fully isolate a folder, only the folder's virtualized content will be available. New elements or modifications of a virtualized element will end up in the sandbox.

Full is mostly used to protect the virtualized application from seeing conflicting elements present on the local machine. Take for example, your virtualized Microsoft Office 2010 having Microsoft Office 2003 locally installed. If you don't protect the virtualized Office from seeing the old local installation of Office, the virtualized Office 2010 will start to self-repair.

To summarize the differences between the isolation modes, refer to the table given as follows:

Isolation mode	System elements	Virtual elements
Merged mode	Application can read and modify content.	Modifications will be sandboxed.
WriteCopy mode	Application can read content. Modifications will be sandboxed.	Modifications will be sandboxed.
Full mode	Application cannot read content.	Modifications will be sandboxed.

You specify different isolation modes for folders using a configuration file named ##Attributes.ini located in each folder, as shown in the following screenshot:

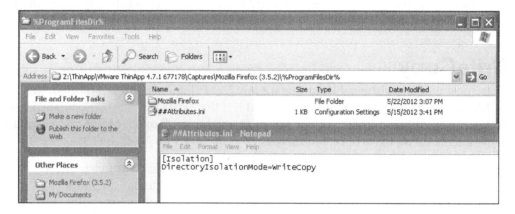

The previous screenshot is an example of WriteCopy specified in the %**ProgramFilesDir**% folder.

In the virtual registry you specify isolation modes in front of the registry sub-tree.

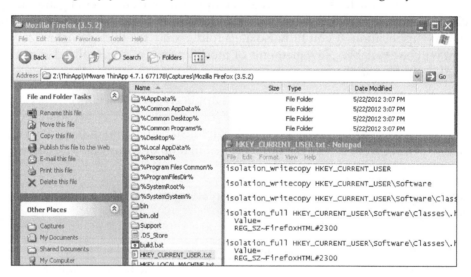

Let's have a look at some isolation mode examples to help you fully understand isolation modes.

Example 1

On your physical machine you have a file called `File.txt` within `C:\Temp folder.`

You have the representation of `C:\Temp` within your project folder where you specify either Merged or WriteCopy as an isolation mode, as shown in the following screenshot:

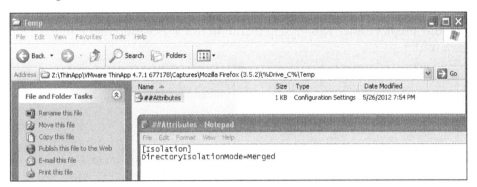

Run your virtualized application (in this example, Mozilla Firefox) and browse to `C:\ Temp`. The application can see the local `File.txt` file, it can open it and read its content.

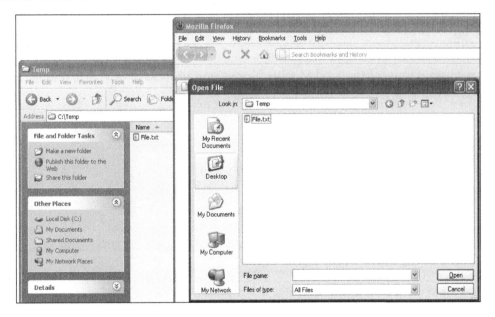

Merged and WriteCopy allows for the virtual environment to read and access native files and registry keys.

Example 2

In the same scenario as the previous example, on your native machine you have
`C:\Temp\File.txt`.

Within your project folder you've specified Full as the isolation mode in the
`C:\Temp` folder.

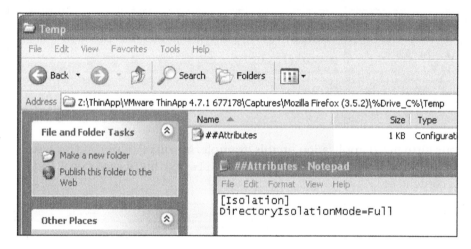

When you run your virtualized Mozilla Firefox and browse to `C:\Temp`, it looks empty, as shown in the following screenshot:

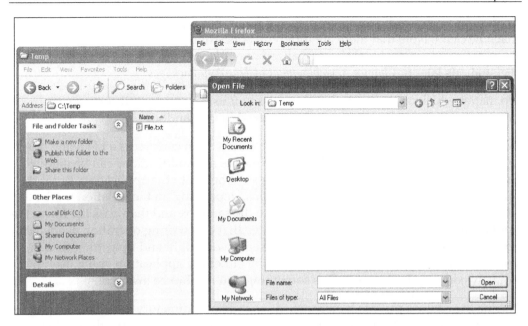

The Full isolation mode hides any native files or registry keys.

Example 3

You are using WriteCopy or Full as your isolation mode on C:\Temp. From within your virtualized application you save a file into C:\Temp. The file will be sandboxed and your native machine is kept clean. Your virtualized application sees the file as being located in C:\Temp.

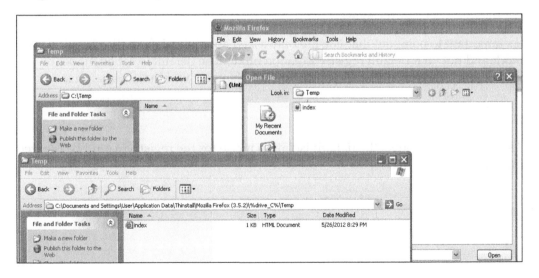

WriteCopy or Full will place new files in the sandbox and keep your physical machine clean. Note that there are different associations for the `.html` file between the native environment and the virtualized one. We will discuss the file type registrations later in *Chapter 3, Deployment of ThinApp Packages*.

No matter which one of the isolation modes you use, if a virtual file or registry key is modified, the modification will be stored in the sandbox.

When does a file end up in the sandbox? An application can access a file using one of two methods. It can be read-only, which means no modifications can be made to the file and the ThinApp runtime simply passes the file to the application. But if the application opens a file for writing operations, depending on the isolation mode, the ThinApp runtime will first copy the file into the sandbox and then pass the file to the application. This way ThinApp can guarantee that any writing operation needed can be done immediately to the file. This also means you might end up getting files in your sandbox that have not been modified by either the application or the user. It's not very common but nevertheless something you need to be aware of.

During the capture process, you're asked what default directory isolation mode you want to use. This is of very little technical importance and is mostly a policy decision. I tend to use WriteCopy as my default isolation mode during packaging and tweaking of the project. This way I know that all I do will be sandboxed. Later, when I compile my production version, I change to Merged as the default directory isolation mode. This way, users are less likely to run into the problem of storing a file somewhere without being able to find the file later on since it has been sandboxed. The default isolation mode is specified within your `Package.ini` file using the following parameter:

```
[Isolation]
DirectoryIsolationMode=
```

It's important to point out that you are only asked about the default directory isolation mode and not your default registry isolation mode. The default isolation mode for your registry is always WriteCopy but you can change it within `Package.ini`.

```
[Isolation]
RegistryIsolationMode=Merged
```

As a result of the above, the default isolation mode for the registry would be Merged instead of WriteCopy.

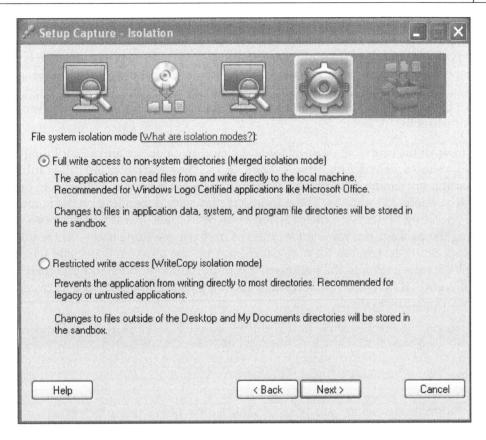

During the capture process you are asked about which default directory isolation mode to use, as shown in the previous screenshot.

The virtual filesystem

ThinApp packagers are working with three different virtual filesystems. The first one is the project folder content. Here, a packager can change the .ini files, replace the old .dll files with new updated ones, and delete or add any files and folders needed. The second virtual filesystem is created when compiling the project; an exact copy of the filesystem found in the project folder will be compiled into the package as a read-only version of the virtual filesystem. There is no way an end user can modify the content of the package. When using the application, a third version of the filesystem is created in the sandbox: the read and write version of the filesystem.

The complete filesystem known to the virtualized application is a combination of the native (physical) filesystem on the machine, the read-only virtual filesystem stored in the package, and the read and write version stored in the sandbox. If there is a conflict between the native filesystem and the virtual one, the virtual environment will win and the virtual file will be the one presented to the application. If there is a conflict between the sandbox content and the read-only filesystem, then the sandbox content will win.

All folders in the root of the project folder (excluding Support and bin folders) are in a variable format, for example, %AppData%. These variables are called **folder macros** and are similar to variables used in the operating system. Folder macros point to predefined locations. These locations may vary depending on the language of the operating system or which version of the Windows operating system you're running the package on. Some folder macros may use the same names as the ones in the operating system but they are different from one another. Especially when using VBScripts built into the packages, it is important to understand that there is a difference. It's the folder macros that allow a package to be portable between different operating systems.

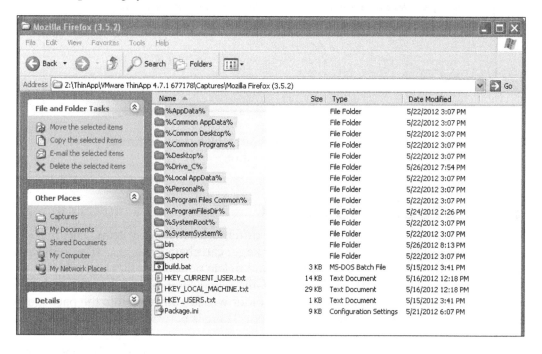

The previous screenshot shows a project folder showing some folder macros.

`%AppData%` refers to the user's roaming profile, which is mostly used to save user settings. Executing a ThinApp package on a Windows XP machine, the `%AppData%` will refer to `C:\Documents and Settings\UserName\Application Data`. Executing the same package on a Windows 7 machine, `%AppData%` will refer to `C:\Users\UserName\AppData\Roaming`. Since ThinApp uses `%AppData%`, the user settings will follow the user no matter which OS the package is executed on.

A list of all folder macros can be found in *References* at the end of this book.

The virtual registry

The virtual registry exists in three versions as well. Within the project folder you will find the virtual registry represented by three clear text files, **HKEY_CURRENT_USER.txt**, **HKEY_LOCAL_MACHINE.txt**, and **HKEY_USERS.txt**.

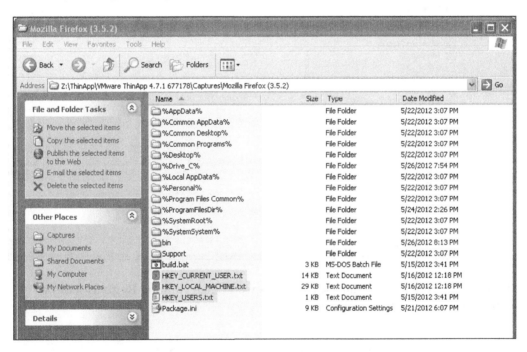

When you run **build.bat** the content of these registry files are compiled into the package as read-only versions. When you use the package, the read and write version is created in the sandbox.

You may ask yourself where **HKEY_CLASSES_ROOT** is. **HKEY_CLASSES_ROOT** is a merged view of HKEY_LOCAL_MACHINE\Software\Classes and HKEY_CURRENT_USER\Software\Classes. **HKEY_CLASSES_ROOT** will be created dynamically during the launch of your package, in a similar way to how the Windows OS generates **HKEY_CLASSES_ROOT** at boot time.

The file database is included in the virtual registry. You can see it while running regedit.exe within your virtual environment.

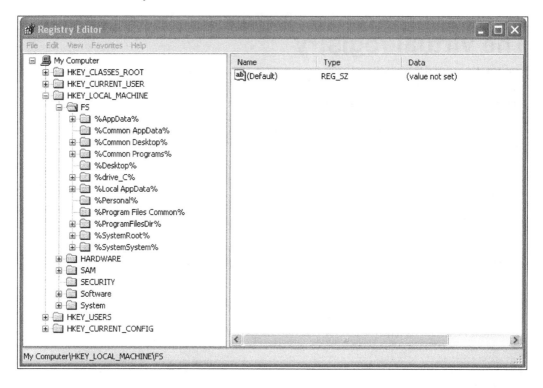

The ThinApp filesystem database can be viewed when running **Registry Editor** within the virtualized environment.

Application Linking (AppLink)

By default, two virtualized applications are isolated from each other. Application One cannot see files or registry entries virtualized in Application Two's package. The ThinApp feature AppLink lets packagers allow full integration between two or more packages. AppLinking packages will effectively merge the different virtualized environments into one big environment. ThinApp supports up to 250 packages linked together but in reality you will never AppLink that many packages together.

There will be a penalty in the startup time for each AppLink and pretty soon your implementation will become too complicated to maintain and manage. Try to limit the amount of AppLinks between five to ten.

AppLink will allow you to package your main application into one package and any dependencies as AppLink. This allows for a more modular design of your desktop environment. A typical use case is a packaged browser and Java, .NET, Active X, Flash as AppLink packages. AppLink is not limited to dependencies. A packaged Microsoft Office and an application tightly integrating with Office can be AppLinked together. This way it will look like both the applications are locally installed on the client, and full integration between applications is possible.

The package your end users launch first is called the parent package. Any AppLink packages are referred to as child packages. There is no difference between a parent and child package. Both are valid, normal ThinApp packages. A package being a child when Application A is launched can just as easily be a parent when you launch it separately. Adobe Acrobat Reader is an excellent example. It can be launched as a separate application but is often a child to your packaged Internet Explorer.

Let's say you packaged Internet Explorer and Adobe Acrobat Reader in two different packages. If you associate .pdf files to your Acrobat Reader Package you will be able to click on a link to a .pdf file from within your virtualized Internet Explorer and a separate Acrobat Reader window will be used to display the Acrobat document. If you want Internet Explorer (IE) to use the embedded Acrobat Reader within the IE window you must AppLink the two packages together. This way Internet Explorer will see Adobe Acrobat Reader as locally installed. The registry keys identifying the embedded functionality in IE will be present in the virtual environment.

When you launch a parent package, its virtual environment will load first, and then the child packages' environments will be merged into the active environment. This happens every time you launch the parent package. If you change the content of a child package the new updated environment will be merged upon the next launch of the parent package. This allows individual updates of your packages. The load order is either alphabetic or in the order specified within `Package.ini`.

The following is an example of an alphabetic load order:

```
[BuildOptions]
OptionalAppLinks=C:\Plugins\*.exe
```

The following is an example of a predefined load order:

```
[BuildOptions]
OptionalAppLinks=C:\Plugins\LoadMeFirst.exe; C:\Plugins\LoadMeLast.exe
```

When you configure AppLink, it is important to understand that you have to point to a data container. It is the virtual environment stored in the data container you want to merge into your running environment. So if your AppLink package uses a separate data container, make sure you refer to the correct file extension, that is, `FileName.dat`.

ThinApp supports one parent package being AppLinked to up to 250 child packages. ThinApp also supports many parent packages AppLinking to one child package. A child package can have its own AppLink, and nested loading of AppLinks is fully supported. This means you could end up launching one parent package, AppLinking to one child package that loads one or more child packages of its own. Pretty soon you risk losing the complete overview of where files and registries are located and which isolation mode is active. A file or a registry key may exist in more than one package in your AppLink chain. In order to resolve these conflicts, the ThinApp runtime will use "last loaded". This means if you have `C:\Temp\File.txt` in your parent package and in your child package, the version in your child package will be used. Parent environments are always loaded first and then child environments are loaded in either alphabetic order or in the load order specified within your `Package.ini` file. What about isolation modes? Here the ThinApp runtime uses a different method, wherein the most restrictive mode will win. This means if your parent package has Merged on the folder `C:\Temp`, then make sure not to use any other isolation modes in any of your child packages. Remember that nested packages will be part of the whole AppLink chain as well. Now it's getting clearer why I recommend using only a small number of AppLink packages in a desktop environment design.

An AppLink package is only loaded once per execution. If you have a complex AppLink chain referring to the same child package multiple times, the child package will be merged only once, the first time it is referred to.

AppLink conflict resolution for isolation modes

- *WriteCopy versus Merged, WriteCopy will win*
- *WriteCopy versus Full, Full will win*

AppLink will discard any sandboxes existing for the child package. Let's say you AppLink to Adobe Acrobat Reader. This package might have been used separately and therefore has the user settings stored within its sandbox. Now, when you execute the parent package, the parent sandbox is the only one in use and any settings stored within the Adobe Acrobat's sandbox will not be part of the running environment.

If your child packages have any virtualized services or VBScripts, they will be active when using AppLink. Bear in mind that, starting services may be a time consuming task. AppLinking to a package starting services might therefore add extra time to the launch time.

ThinApp supports the following two flavors of AppLink:

- Optional AppLink
- Required AppLink.

Optional AppLink

When using the dynamic AppLink called `OptionalAppLinks` in `Package.ini`, the package will AppLink to any package available. If no AppLink can be found, the package will happily launch anyway.

Using Optional AppLink offers a true dynamic design of your applications. You don't even have to know upon packaging if you need to AppLink or not. Simply activate `OptionalAppLinks` and you can always add functionality to your package later on.

The following are example configurations:

```
[BuildOptions]
OptionalAppLinks=plugins\*.exe
```

The result of this configuration is that, any package located in the folder called `plugins` relative to the parent package itself will be added.

```
[BuildOptions]
OptionalAppLinks=plugins\*.exe; plugins\*.dat
```

The result of this configuration is that, any package located in the `plugins` folder relative to the parent package will be AppLinked, including separate data containers.

```
[BuildOptions]
OptionalAppLinks=\\ServerName\ShareName\MyAppLinks\Java.dat
```

The result of this configuration is that the Java package located on a network share will be AppLinked.

```
[BuildOptions]
OptionalAppLinks=C:\Program Files\Java 1.6 (VMware ThinApp)\*.exe; C:\
Program Files\Flash (VMware ThinApp)\*.exe
```

The result of this configuration is that, if available, a virtualized Java and locally deployed Flash clients will be AppLinked. This is a very common AppLink configuration used when you deploy ThinApps with the help of MSI and existing deployment tools. We will get back to some different deployment scenarios later.

```
[BuildOptions]
OptionalAppLinks=%HOMEPATH%\*\*.exe
```

This configuration shows that, AppLink supports environment variables and wildcard searches. This example will search one folder deep in the users %HOMEPATH% for child packages called *.exe.

```
[BuildOptions]
OptionalAppLinks=\\ServerName\ShareName\*\*\*.dat
```

In this configuration, ThinApp will search two folders deep for child packages named *.dat. For example, both \\ServerName\ShareName\AppLinks\Java\ java.dat and \\ServerName\ShareName\AppLinks\Flash\Flash.dat will be AppLinked.

Required AppLink

Required AppLink, called RequiredAppLinks in Package.ini, will deny execution of the package if the AppLink cannot be found. When you use a required AppLink, make sure you specify the whole filename of your child packages. You should not use the wildcard (*) since this will effectively disable the required rule set, that is, deny usage of the parent package if AppLink packages are not available.

```
[BuildOptions]
RequiredAppLinks=C:\Program Files\Java 1.6 (VMware ThinApp)\java.exe;
C:\Program Files\Flash (VMware ThinApp)\flash.exe
```

This configuration means that the Java and Flash packages will be AppLinked. If they are not accessible, the user will be denied the ability to run the parent package.

```
[BuildOptions]
RequiredAppLinks=\\ServerName\ShareName\java.exe
```

This configuration means that the Java package located on a network share will be AppLinked. If the Java package is not accessible, the user will be denied the ability to run the parent package.

The ThinApp utilities folder and its content

The ThinApp utilities folder is installed in `C:\Program Files\VMware\VMware ThinApp` by default. Only the ThinApp packagers need access to the ThinApp utilities folder - end users never need access to it. If desired, you can move this folder to a network share and run all the tools from there. The ThinApp utilities are virtualized using ThinApp so the folder is just as portable as any ThinApp package. Placing the folder on a network share makes it easier to access the tools from any machine. Often when packaging, you are using virtual machines and reverting the virtual machines to clean states between each capture. Having the ThinApp utilities folder on a network share will make them easier to maintain. Changing the version of ThinApp used does not require a new snapshot of your virtual machine. Another benefit is that all your packager colleagues can share one and the same ThinApp utilities folder and settings.

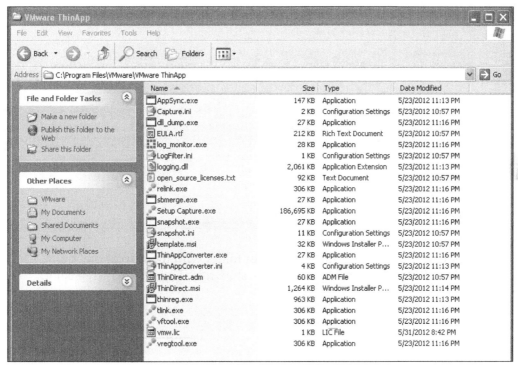

Default location of the ThinApp utilities Folder.

If you don't place the ThinApp utilities folder in the default location, you should make sure that you specify an environment variable called **THINSTALL_BIN** pointing to the ThinApp utilities folder. This way the `build.bat` file will find the location of the tools needed while building your project folder. Using the **THINSTALL_BIN** environment variable allows you to have multiple versions of the ThinApp utilities folder present. You can switch between active folders by simply changing the value of the environment variable.

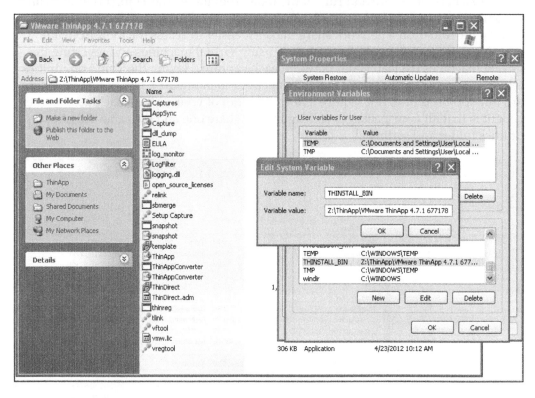

Specify the location of your ThinApp utilities folder with the help of the **THINSTALL_BIN** environment variable, as shown in the previous screenshot.

Let's have a look at some of the files you'll find within the ThinApp utilities folder. Most of them will be discussed in much more detail later in this book. The following are the files present:

- `AppSync.exe`

  AppSync is one of the built-in update mechanisms within ThinApp. We will cover AppSync more in depth later in this book. Running **AppSync.exe** allows you to specify a package to AppSync and an AppSync URL, where the update is located, providing a more dynamic method of updating the deployed ThinApp packages than the AppSync you can configure using `package.ini`.

  `log_monitor.exe`.

  The **log monitor** is a trace tool used to troubleshoot ThinApp packages.

- `Capture.ini` and `LogFilter.ini`

  These are filter files used to filter what is captured while running the log monitor.

- `relink.exe`

  Relink is used to inject a new runtime, certain settings, and a license key into an existing package without the need to completely rebuild the whole project folder.

- `sbmerge.exe`

  Sbmerge stands for **sandbox merge**. It is a tool used by packagers to merge the content of a sandbox into an existing project folder. It is a great tool used to apply changes and updates to a project. Running `sbmerge.exe` without any switches will display the `help` file.

- `Setup Capture.exe`

  Setup Capture is the tool used to capture an application installation and create a project folder. Within **Setup Capture** you can specify your license key and if you want to change the license key or "licensed to" name, you must change these within **Setup Capture** and then rebuild your project or run relink on the packages.

You change the license key and "Licensed to" information by launching **Setup Capture**, clicking on the top-left corner and choosing **License**, as shown in the following screenshot:

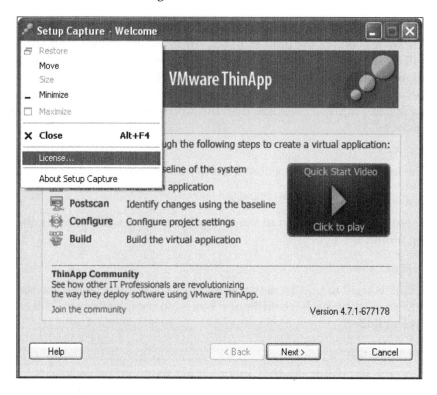

You are now shown the **Enter License Key** dialog box, as in the following screenshot:

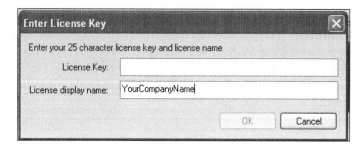

Type in your license key and licensed display name. Click on **OK** and then **Cancel** in the **Setup Capture** main window. You have now successfully updated the license information. Simply rebuild your project to update your packages or run `relink.exe`.

- `snapshot.exe`

  This is the ThinApp snapshot tool. Running `snapshot.exe` from a command prompt allows you to capture an installation and create a project folder without running **Setup Capture**. Running `snapshot.exe` without any switches will give you the full `help` file. The following procedure will create a project folder using `snapshot.exe`:

  1. Run the command `snapshot.exe c:\PreScan.snapshot`.
  2. Install the application.
  3. Run `snapshot.exe c:\PostScan.snapshot`.
  4. Run `snapshot.exe c:\PreScan.snapshot -SuggestName c:\PostScan.snapshot`.
  5. Run the command `snapshot.exe c:\PreScan.snapshot -Diff c:\PostScan.snapshot c:\ProjectFolder`.
  6. Run `snapshot.exe c:\PreScan.snapshot -SuggestProject c:\PostScan.snapshot c:\OutputTemplate.ini`.
  7. Run `snapshot.exe c:\OutputTemplate.ini -GenerateProject c:\ProjectFolder`.

- `snapshot.ini`

  `Snapshot.ini` is the exclusion list used by **Setup Capture** and `snapshot.exe`. Here you can specify parts of the operating system that should not be scanned during the capturing process. The defaults are implemented to keep your project from capturing unnecessary content. It's not recommended to have an antivirus software installed on your capturing machine, but if policy dictates that you must, you can use the `snapshot.ini` file to exclude locations for the antivirus log files and such. This keeps the changes from being a part of the captured environment and thereby polluting your project folder.

- `template.msi`

  ThinApp can generate an MSI file to simplify the deployment of the ThinApp packages. Using an MSI file will allow the use of any existing deployment tool to distribute ThinApp packages. The MSI files that ThinApp generates are supported by any tool supporting MSI files but are not normal MSI files. ThinApp supports MSI files greater than 2 GB without the use of CAB files. This is accomplished with the help of virtualization within the MSI itself. You cannot use tools such as Orca to modify the MSI properties, since it will destroy the content of the MSI when saved. In order to change the MSI that ThinApp generates, you have to tweak the `template.msi` file instead. Changes applied to the `template.msi` (using Orca or any other tool) file will be incorporated into the MSI files that ThinApp generates.

- `ThinApp.ini`

  `ThinApp.ini` contains the **Setup Capture** user settings, for example, the options to build or skip build at the end of the capture process.

- `ThinAppConverter.exe` and `ThinAppConverter.ini`

  ThinApp Converter is a tool introduced in Version 4.6. With the help of ThinApp Converter and its configuration file `ThinAppConverter.ini`, you can automate the capturing process. This was an early version of automation and is more or less replaced with the tool called **ThinApp Factory**. ThinApp Converter drives the capture process by running virtual machines hosted on ESX or VMware Workstation. `ThinAppConverter.ini` is pretty much the only documentation available for this tool. There are third-party tools using ThinApp Converter to automatically convert installers into ThinApp project format. Quest ChangeBASE is one such tool using ThinApp Converter.

- `ThinDirect.msi` and `ThinDirect.adm`

  ThinDirect is a browser helper you install locally on your client. It will add itself as a browser helper to your local Internet Explorer and allows for automated redirection of URLs to specific packaged browsers. `ThinDirect.msi` is the standalone installer you use to deploy the browser helper. `ThinDirect.adm` is used to add Group Policy Management to your ThinDirect implementation. `ThinDirect.adm` includes five different browsers and 25 different URLs for each one. You can change the amount of supported browsers or URLs simply by editing the file in a text editor.

- `thinreg.exe`

  `Thinreg.exe` is a standalone tool that you can copy to any location. Most of the other tools in the ThinApp utilities must reside within the ThinApp utilities folder to function. `Thinreg.exe` is used to register a package on a client machine, offering the look and feel of a locally-installed application. By registering a package, you can add shortcuts onto your desktop or the **Start** menu and you can register file extensions, protocols, and object types to a package. Run `thinreg.exe` without any arguments for the `help` file.

- `tlink.exe`, `vftool.exe`, and `vregtool.exe`

  `tlink.exe`, `vftool.exe`, and `vregtool.exe` are all used to compile your project folder into a virtualized package. `Build.bat` calls these files. `Vregtool.exe` can also be used to investigate the registry changes located in the sandbox. Running `vregtool.exe` without any switches will show you the `help` file.

Summary

In this chapter we learned the basics of application virtualization, isolation modes, the sandbox, application linking, and we looked at the ThinApp utilities folder. In the next chapter we will cover the packaging process in more detail.

2
Application Packaging

In this chapter we will cover the packaging process. We'll discuss packaging's best practices the, packaging environment, entry points, the data container, and `Package.ini`.

By the end of this chapter, you will have learned about:

- How to capture an application
- Entry points and the data container
- How your packaging environment affects your packages
- Packaging Internet Explorer
- VBScript support within ThinApp
- Package.ini

Packaging

Packaging an application means collecting all of the required files and registry keys in one easy-to-deploy container. Different packaging formats have different containers. The most common method, MSI, has been around for ages. When you deploy a legacy MSI package, the application's files will be copied onto the local hard disk. Components such as DLLs will be registered, and the registry will be modified. Most modern applications are already packaged on delivery. MSI is very common but different formats exist that use `.exe` files as their container. Most enterprises repackage their applications. In this way settings can be customized and features can be turned on or off. Even though there are software vendors that use application virtualization, a clear majority of them use legacy, natively installed packaging formats as their installers.

Application virtualization captures all changes made by a legacy installer. When you execute the virtualized package, the application thinks it is locally installed but all changes made by the installer are actually virtualized and only available within the virtual environment. Application virtualization means you can never install the application – you simply execute the application. The fact that you don't have to install the application has many advantages, but it also comes with a few challenges. We will cover as much as possible of both in this book, to make sure you avoid the most common traps.

Running the Setup Capture wizard

Let's capture our first application together. The first couple of applications you capture should be easy ones. There's no point starting with the toughest possible application. One of the easiest applications to start with is Mozilla Firefox. If you do not currently own ThinApp, you can download a fully functional trial version from VMware's home page, http://www.vmware.com/thinapp. The trial version will generate time-bombed packages but the project folders it creates are fully functional and a simple rebuild, using a licensed copy of ThinApp, will produce unlimited packages. The following steps will help you capture our first application:

1. Have a virtual machine available as your capturing environment. Personally I use VMware Fusion but any virtualization solution should work. Boot your capturing machine. I'm using Windows XP in this example but you should be able to run through the example using Windows 7 as well. Before doing anything else make sure you have a clean snapshot of your virtual machine. This way you are able to revert into a clean state after installation and capture of the application.

2. Start **Setup Capture**. (Setup Capture.exe found in the ThinApp Utilities folder).

3. Click on **Next**.

4. Click on **Prescan>** to start your pre-installation snapshot.

5. When the pre-installation snapshot is created, it is time to install your application. This is shown in the following screenshot:

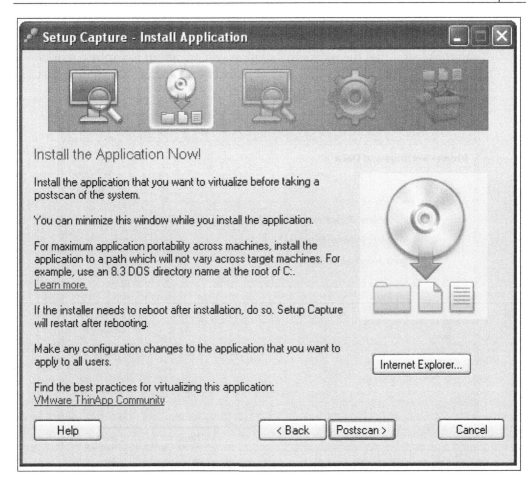

6. Minimize the **Setup Capture** wizard.

7. Start the **Mozilla Firefox** setup.

8. Run through the installation of your application.

9. If the application does not register its license during the first launch, it's recommended to always launch the application at least once. This way you can make sure that the native installation you are about to capture works as expected. Mozilla Firefox does not register any licenses during the first launch so I should launch it at least once.

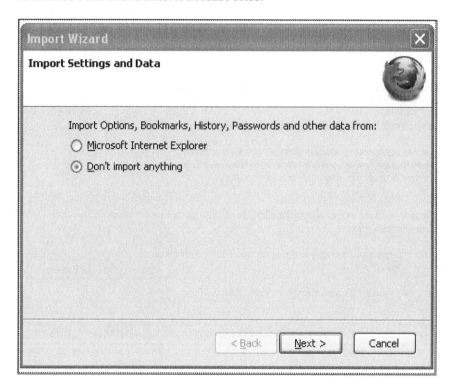

10. By launching the application, you can complete the initial application setup.

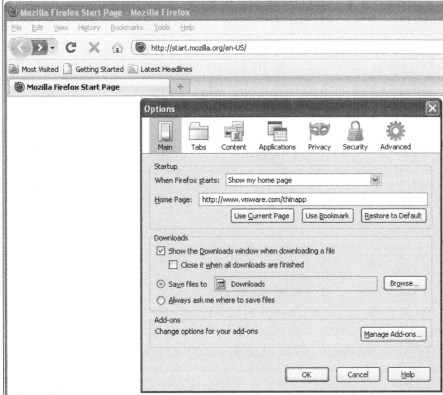

11. Customize the application to fit your organization. All modifications will be captured and preserved by ThinApp.

12. Close Mozilla Firefox.

13. Go back to the **Setup Capture** wizard.

14. Click on **Postscan>**.

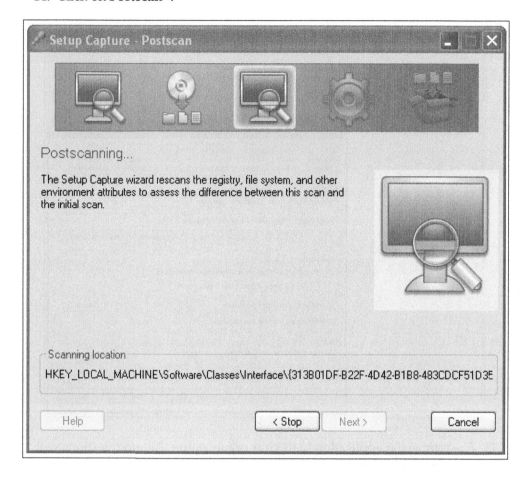

The postscan operation can take a while depending on how much has been changed.

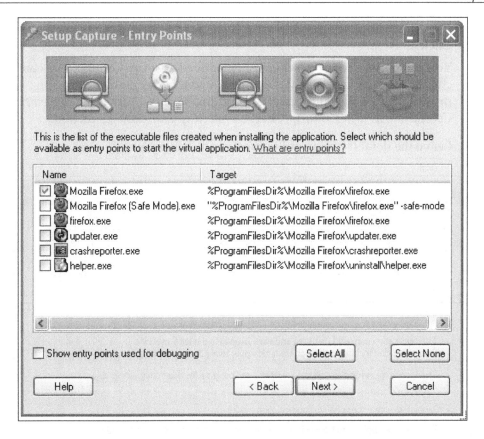

When the post-installation scan is finished, you are presented with a list of all new executable, batch files and control panel objects. The objects with shortcuts are the ones that are activated by default. In the previous screenshot, I disabled the **Mozilla Firefox (Safe Mode)** entry point because I do not need it. ThinApp supports hardcoded switches as well as passing switches into the virtual environment. If you launch an entry point with a switch, the ThinApp runtime will take the switch and pass it onto the target executable.

15. Uncheck the **Mozilla Firefox (Safe Mode).exe** entry point.

16. Click on **Next**.

Next you can activate management using **VMware Horizon Application Manager**. You can find more on Horizon's capabilities of managing ThinApp packages in *Chapter 3, Deployment of ThinApp Packages*.

17. Leave **Manage with VMware Horizon Application Manager** unchecked.

18. Click on **Next**.

    You can protect your packages using Active Directory Groups. You can change this later in `Package.ini` within your project folder. More on protecting your packages can be found in *Chapter 6, Design and Implementation Considerations using ThinApp*, in the *Protecting your packages* section.

19. Leave the default option of **Everyone** and click on **Next**.

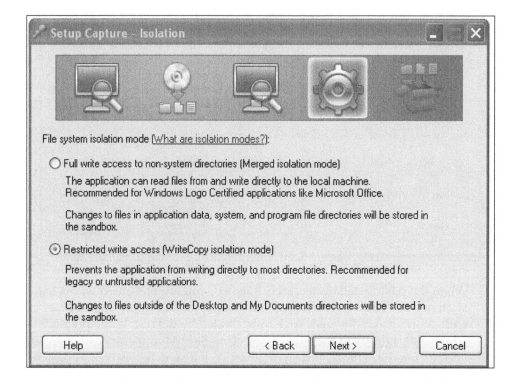

The default filesystem isolation mode you choose is of very little technical importance. If your application requires a specific isolation mode on a certain location, then you should specify this in your project folder and not rely on the default setting. More details on isolation modes can be found in the *Isolation Modes* section in *Chapter 1, Application Virtualization*. The default filesystem isolation mode is only used when no isolation mode has been specified. Note that the question only concerns the filesystem. The default isolation mode for the registry is always WriteCopy. When packaging an application, I always choose WriteCopy as my default isolation mode. This way I'm sure to capture all the changes made by the package in my sandbox.

I would probably run the package a couple of times and I would want to get to know the application and what it modifies. Using WriteCopy as my default isolation mode, I can investigate the sandbox to learn what the application modifies. When I'm ready to build my production version of the package, I'm likely to choose Merged as my default filesystem isolation mode. That way I don't run the risk of users storing their documents on a location that is sandboxed by mistake. Imagine the frustration an end user experiences when saving a document into the root of C: and not finding it there because it got sandboxed.

20. Choose the WriteCopy isolation mode and click on **Next**.

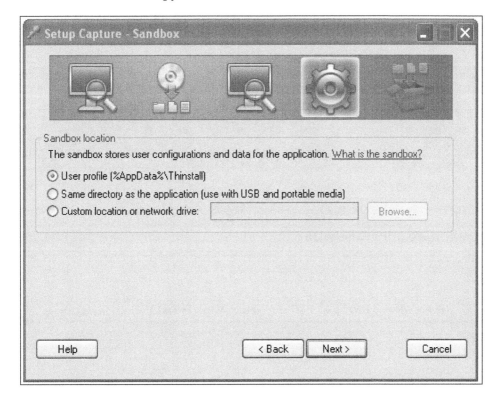

If my production environment uses a different sandbox location than the default, I will change this at the end of packaging an application. When conducting tests, I prefer to keep the sandbox on the local machine for easy access.

21. Leave the **Sandbox location** option at **User profile** and click on **Next**.

    ThinApp packages can deliver reports to a VMware server. This way VMware can not only learn about the applications that generate support calls but also see which applications are successfully running virtualized with the help of ThinApp. The reports are made completely anonymously.

22. Click on **Next**.

    When **Setup Capture** recognizes that you are capturing a browser, it will ask if you would like to specify ThinDirect URLs. Here you can list URLs that should be handled by this virtualized browser. Find more on ThinDirect in the *Virtualizing Internet Explorer 6* section of this chapter.

23. Leave the ThinDirect list empty and click on **Next**.

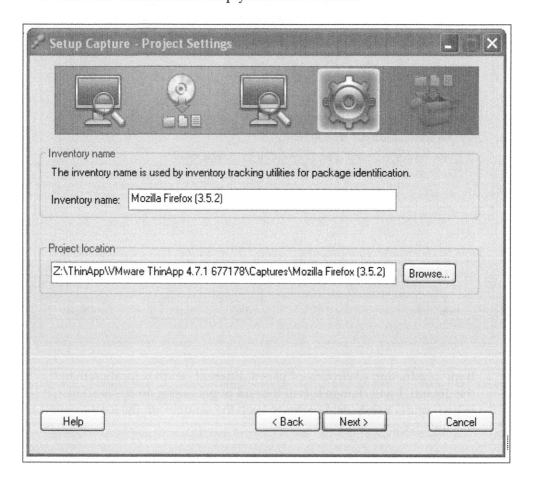

Next you're asked about **Inventory name** and where to store your project folder. Choose a suitable name. The Inventory name will be used to prepopulate parameters such as `SandboxName` in `Package.ini`. All parameters can of course be changed later on. Please be aware of the path length of your project location. It's often wise to choose a much shorter path than in my previous example. It all depends on the folder structure of the application you are capturing. Many times you will hit the built-in character length limitation within the operating system. A good practice is to store your project folders in the root of a network share. Another method of getting a short path is to use `SUBST` to map a folder as a drive letter.

24. Click on **Next**.

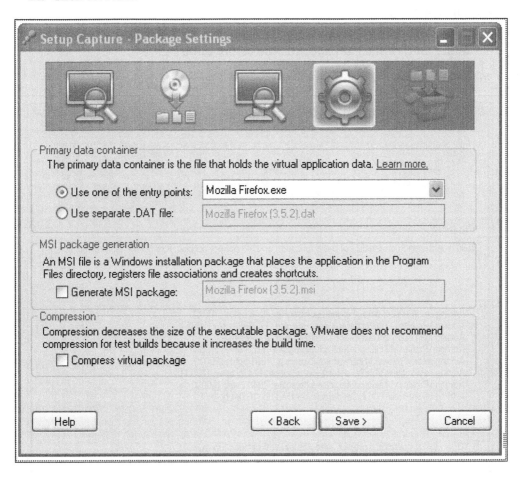

The next step is where you decide where to store your virtual environment. The virtual environment container is called a **data container**. The data container can either be a separate file or an entry point. You can choose among the active entry points. You can easily change the data container and its name within the `Package.ini` file. More information can be found in the section called *Entry points and* the *data container* later in this chapter. You can choose to generate an MSI file for easy deployment of your package using existing deployment tools. You can also choose to compress the files within your package. Both of these options add to your build time so if I wanted to use either one I wouldn't switch them on until later when I build my production package.

25. Click on **Save**.

   Your project folder is now created. You have the option to view your project folder and/or the `Package.ini` file before building.

26. Click on **Build** to compile your project folder into a package.

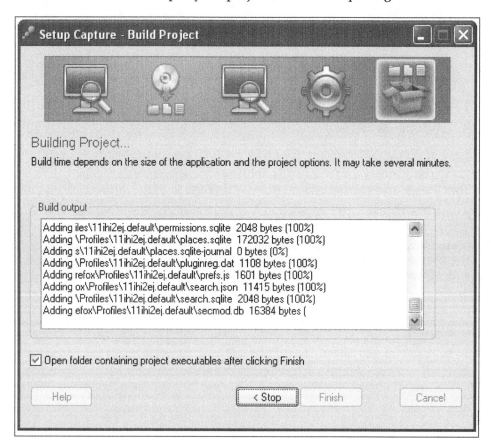

Building your package may take a while. The time it takes depends on the size of your project folder and if you use compression or not.

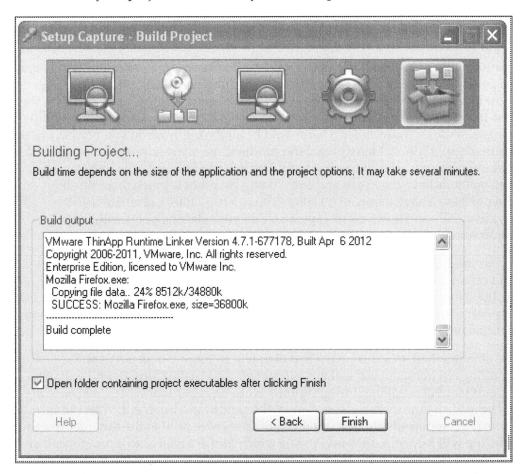

27. Click on **Finish** to close **Setup Capture** and open the `bin` folder containing the package you just created.

Congratulations! You have created your first ThinApp package. In order to test your package, make sure you have saved the project folder outside your virtual machine. Revert to a clean snapshot of your virtual machine and run the package. Packaged Mozilla Firefox should run on pretty much any Windows version, ranging from Windows XP to Windows 7. 32-bit or 64-bit shouldn't matter.

The capture and build environment

You cannot write a book about a packaging format without discussing the environment used to create the packages. The environment you use to capture an installation is of great importance.

ThinApp uses a method of **snapshotting** when capturing an application installation. This means you create a snapshot (**Pre-Installation Snapshot**) of the current state of the machine. After modifying the environment, you create another snapshot, the **Post-Installation Snapshot**. The differences between the two snapshots represent the changes made by the installer. This should be all the information you need in order to run the application. Many packaging products use snapshotting as a method of capturing changes. The alternative would be to try to hook into the installer itself. Both methods have their pros and cons. Using snapshot is much more flexible. You don't even have to run an installer. You can copy files and create registry keys manually and it will all be captured. But, your starting point will decide the outcome.

If your machine already contains the **Java Runtime Environment** (**JRE**) and the application you are capturing requires Java, then you will not be able to capture the JRE. Since it was already there when you ran the pre-install snapshot, it will not be a part of the captured differences. This means your package would require Java installed or it will fail to run. The package will not be self-contained.

The other method, monitoring the installer, will be more independent of the capturing environment but will not support all the installer formats and will not support manual tweaking during capture. Nothing is black or white. Snapshotting can be made a little more independent of the capture environment. When an installer discovers components already installed, it can register itself to the same components. ThinApp will recognize this, investigate which files are related to a component, and mark them as needed to be included in the package. But this is not a bulletproof method. So the general rule is to make sure your environment allows ThinApp to capture all required dependencies of the application.

ThinApp packages are able to support multiple operating systems with one single package. This is a great feature and really helps in lowering the overall administration of maintaining an application. The possibility of running the same package on your Windows XP clients, Windows 7 machines, and your XenApp servers is unique. Most other packaging formats require you to maintain one package per environment.

The easiest method to package an application is to capture it on the platform where it will run. Normally you can achieve an out of the box success rate of 60 – 80 percent. This means you have not tweaked the project in any way. The package might not be ready for production but it will run on a clean machine not having the application locally installed.

If you want to support multiple operating systems you should choose the lowest platform you need to support. Most of the time this would be Windows XP. From ThinApp's point of view, Windows XP and Windows Server 2003 are of the same generation and Windows 7 and Windows 2008 R2 are of the same generation.

Most installers are environment aware. They will investigate the targeting platform and if it discovers a Windows 7 operating system, it knows that some files are already present in the same or newer version than required. Installing on a Windows XP with no service pack would force those required files to be installed locally, and therefore captured by the capturing process. Having these files captured from an installation made on Windows XP rarely conflicts the running of the application on Windows 7 and helps you achieve multiple OS support.

Creating a package for one single operating system is of course the easiest task. Creating a package supporting multiple operating systems, all being 32-bit systems is a little harder. How hard depends on the application. Creating a package supporting many different OS and both 32-bit and 64-bit versions is the hardest. But it is doable. It just requires a little extra packaging effort. Some applications cannot run on a 64-bit OS, but most applications offer some kind of work around. If the application contains 16-bit code, then it's impossible to make it run on a 64-bit environment. 64-bit environments cannot handle 16-bit code. Your only workaround for those scenarios is whole machine virtualization technologies. VMware Workstation, VMware View, Citrix XenDesktop, Microsoft Med-V, and many others offer you the capability to access a virtualized 32-bit operating system on your 64-bit machine.

In general, you should use an environment that is as clean as possible. This will guarantee that all your packages include as many dependencies as possible, making them portable and robust. But it's not written in stone. If you are capturing an add-on to Microsoft Office, then Microsoft Office has to be locally installed in your capturing environment or the add-on installer would fail to run. You must design your capture environment to allow flexibility. Sometimes you capture on Windows XP, the next application might be captured on Windows 7 64-bit. The next day you'll capture on a machine having JRE installed, or Microsoft Office. The use of virtual machines is a must. Physical machines are supported but the hours spent on reverting to a clean state to start the capture of the next application makes it virtually useless.

My capture environment is my MacBook Pro running VMware Fusion and several virtual machines such as Windows XP, Windows Vista, Windows 7, Windows 2003 Server, and of course Windows Server 2008. All VMs have several snapshots (states of the virtual machine) so I can easily jump back and forth between clean, Microsoft Office-installed and different service packs and browsers. Yes, it will require some serious disk space. I'm always low on free disk space. No matter how big the disks you buy are, your project folders and virtual machines will eat it all. I have two disks in my MacBook. One SSD disk, where I keep most of my virtual machines, and one traditional hard disk where I keep all my project folders. The best capture environments I've ever seen have been hosted on VMware vSphere and ESX. Using server hardware to run client operating systems make them fast as lightning. Snapshotting of your VMs take seconds, as well as reverting snapshots.

Access to the virtual machines hosted on VMware ESX can be achieved using a console within the vSphere client or basic RDP. The only downside I can see to using an ESX environment is that you cannot do packaging offline, while traveling.

The next logical question is if my capture machine should be a domain member or standalone, this depends, I always prefer to capture on standalone machines. This way I know that group policies will not mess with my capture process. No restrictions will be blocking me from doing what I need to do. But again, sometimes you can simply not capture an application without having access to a backend infrastructure. Then your capture machine must be on the corporate network and most of the time it means that it has to be a domain member. If possible, try putting the machine in a special **Organizational Unit (OU)** where you limit the amount of restrictions.

If at all possible, make sure you don't have antivirus installed on your capturing environment. I know that some enterprises have strict policies forcing even packaging machines to be protected by antivirus. But be careful. There is no way of telling what your antivirus may decide to do to your application's installation and the whole capture process. Most installer manuals clearly state to disable any antivirus during installation. They do that for a reason. Antivirus scanning logs and all that follows will also pollute your project folder. It will probably not break your package but I am a strong believer in delivering clean and optimized packages. So having an antivirus means you will have to spend some time cleaning up your project folders. Alternatively, you can include areas where the antivirus changes content in `snapshot.ini`, the **Setup Capture** exclusion list.

Entry points and the data container

An **entry point** is the doorway into the virtual environment for the end users. An entry point specifies what will be launched within the virtual environment. Mostly an entry point points to an executable, for example, winword.exe. But an entry point doesn't have to point to an executable. You can point an entry point to whatever kind of file you want, as long as the file type has a file association made to it. Whatever is associated to the file type will be launched within the virtual environment. If no file type association exists, you will get the standard operating system dialog box, asking you which application to open the file with. The name of the entry point must use an .exe extension. When the user double-clicks on an entry point, we are asking the operating system to execute the ThinApp runtime. Entry points are managed in Package.ini. You'll find them at the end of the Package.ini file.

The **data container** is the file where ThinApp stores the whole virtual environment and the ThinApp runtime. There can only be one data container per project. The content in the data container is an exact copy of the representation of the virtual environment found in your project folder. The data in the data container is in read-only format. It's the packagers who change the content by rebuilding the project. An end user cannot change the content of the data container. An entry point can be a data container. **Setup Capture** will recommend not using an entry point as a data container if **Setup Capture** believes that the package will be large (200 MB-300 MB). The reason for this is that the icon of the entry point may take up to 20 minutes to be displayed. This is a *feature* of the operating system and there's nothing you can do about it. It's therefore better to store the data container in a separate file and keep your entry points small. Make sure the icons are displayed quickly. **Setup Capture** will force you to use a separate data container when the size is calculated to be larger than 1.5 GB. Windows has a size limitation for executable files. Windows will deny executing a .exe file larger than 2 GB.

The name of the data container can be anything. You will not have to name it with the .dat extension. It doesn't have to have a file extension at all. If you're using a separate data container, you must keep the data container in the same folder as your entry points.

Let's take a closer look at the data container and entry point section of `Package.ini`. You'll find the data container and entry points at the end of the `Package.ini` file. The following is an example `Package.ini` file from a virtualized Mozilla Firefox:

```
[Mozilla Firefox.exe]
Source=%ProgramFilesDir%\Mozilla Firefox\firefox.exe
;ChangeReadOnlyData to bin\Package.ro.tvr to build with old
versions(4.6.0 or earlier) of tools
ReadOnlyData=Package.ro.tvr
WorkingDirectory=%ProgramFilesDir%\Mozilla Firefox
FileTypes=.htm.html.shtml.xht.xhtml
Protocols=FirefoxURL;ftp;http;https
Shortcuts=%Desktop%;%Programs%\Mozilla Firefox;%AppData%\Microsoft\
Internet Explorer\Quick Launch

[Mozilla Firefox (Safe Mode).exe]
Disabled=1
Source=%ProgramFilesDir%\Mozilla Firefox\firefox.exe
Shortcut=Mozilla Firefox.exe
WorkingDirectory=%ProgramFilesDir%\Mozilla Firefox
CommandLine="%ProgramFilesDir%\Mozilla Firefox\firefox.exe" -safe-mode
Shortcuts=%Programs%\Mozilla Firefox
```

A step-by-step explanation for the parameters is given as follows:

```
[Mozilla Firefox.exe]
```

Within [] is the name of the entry point. This is the name the end user will see. Make sure to use `.exe` as your file extension.

```
Source=%ProgramFilesDir%\Mozilla Firefox\firefox.exe
```

The source parameter points to the target of the entry point, that is, what will be launched when the user clicks on the entry point. The source can either be a virtualized or physical file. The target will be launched within the virtual environment no matter where it lives.

```
ReadOnlyData=Package.ro.tvr
```

The `ReadOnlyData` indicates this entry point is in fact a data container as well.

```
WorkingDirectory=%ProgramFilesDir%\Mozilla Firefox
```

This specifies the working directory for the executable launched. This is often a very important parameter. If you do not specify a working directory, the active working directory will be the location of your package. A lot of software depends on having their working directory set to the application's own folder in the program files directory.

```
FileTypes=.htm.html.shtml.xht.xhtml
```

This is used when registering the entry point. It specifies which file extensions should be associated with this entry point. The previous example registers .htm, .html, and so on to the virtualized Mozilla Firefox.

```
Protocols=FirefoxURL;ftp;http;https
```

This is used when registering the entry point. It specifies which protocols should be associated with this entry point. The previous example registers http, https, and so on to the virtualized Mozilla Firefox.

```
Shortcuts=%Desktop%;%Programs%\Mozilla Firefox
```

The parameter Shortcuts is also used when registering your entry points. The Shortcuts parameter decides where shortcuts will be created. The previous example creates shortcuts to virtualized Mozilla Firefox on the **Start** menu in a folder called Mozilla Firefox, as well as a shortcut on the user's desktop.

```
[Mozilla Firefox (Safe Mode).exe]
Disabled=1
```

Disabled means this entry point will not be created during the build of your project.

```
Source=%ProgramFilesDir%\Mozilla Firefox\firefox.exe
Shortcut=Mozilla Firefox.exe
```

Shortcut tells this entry point what its data container is named. If you change the data container's name you will have to change the Shortcut parameter on all entry points using the data container.

```
WorkingDirectory=%ProgramFilesDir%\Mozilla Firefox
CommandLine="%ProgramFilesDir%\Mozilla Firefox\firefox.exe" -safe-mode
```

CommandLine will allow you to specify hardcoded parameters to the executable. It's the native parameters supported by the virtualized application that you use.

```
Shortcuts=%Programs%\Mozilla Firefox
```

There are many more parameters related to entry points. The following are some more examples with descriptions:

```
[Microsoft Office Enterprise 2007.dat]
Source=%ProgramFilesDir%\Microsoft Office\Office12\OSA.EXE
;ChangeReadOnlyData to bin\Package.ro.tvr to build with old
versions(4.6.0 or earlier) of tools
ReadOnlyData=Package.ro.tvr
MetaDataContainerOnly=1
```

> `MetaDataContainer` indicates that this is a separate data container.

```
[Microsoft Office Excel 2007.exe]
Source=%ProgramFilesDir%\Microsoft Office\Office12\EXCEL.EXE
Shortcut=Microsoft Office Enterprise 2007.dat
FileTypes=.csv.dqy.iqy.slk.xla.xlam.xlk.xll.xlm.xls.xlsb.xlshtml.xlsm.
xlsx.xlt.xlthtml.xltm.xltx.xlw
Comment=Perform calculations, analyze information, and visualize data
in spreadsheets by using Microsoft Office Excel.
```

> `Comment` allows you to specify text to be displayed when hovering your mouse over the shortcut to the entry point.

```
ObjectTypes=Excel.Addin;Excel.AddInMacroEnabled;Excel.
Application;Excel.Application.12;Excel.Backup;Excel.Chart;Excel.
Chart.8;Excel.CSV;Excel.Macrosheet;Excel.Sheet;Excel.Sheet.12;Excel.
Sheet.8;Excel.SheetBinaryMacroEnabled;Excel.SheetBinaryMacroEnab
led.12;Excel.SheetMacroEnabled;Excel.SheetMacroEnabled.12;Excel.
SLK;Excel.Template;Excel.Template.8;Excel.TemplateMacroEnabled;Excel.
Workspace;Excel.XLL
```

> This specifies the object types which will be registered to the entry point when registered.

```
Shortcuts=%Programs%\Microsoft Office
StatusBarDisplayName=WordProcessor
```

> Users can change the name displayed in the ThinApp splash screen. In this example, `WordProcessor` will be displayed as the title.

```
Icon=%ProgramFilesDir%\Microsoft Office\Office12\EXCEL.ico
```

> `Icon` allows you to specify an icon for your entry point. Most of the times ThinApp will display the correct icon without this parameter. You can point to an executable to use its built-in icons as well. You can specify a different icon set by applying 1 or 2 and so on to the icon path, for example, `Icon=%ProgramFilesDir%\Microsoft Office\Office12\EXCEL.EXE,1`

The most common entry points should be either `cmd.exe` or `regedit.exe`. You'll find them in all `Package.ini` files but they are disabled by default. Since `cmd.exe` and `regedit.exe` most likely weren't modified during **Setup Capture**, they are not part of the virtual environment. So the source will be the native `cmd.exe` and `regedit.exe`. These two entry points are the packagers' best friends. Using these entry points allows a packager to investigate the environment known to the virtualized application. What you can see using `cmd.exe` or `regedit.exe` is what the application sees. This is a great help when troubleshooting.

If you package an add-on to a natively installed application, the typical example is packaging JRE and you want the local Internet Explorer to be able to use it. Creating an entry point within your Java package using native Internet Explorer as a source, is a perfect method of dealing with it. Now you can offer a separate shortcut to the user, allowing users to choose when to use native Java or when to use virtualized Java. ThinApp's isolation will allow virtualization of one Java version running on a machine with another version natively installed. The only problem with this approach is how you educate your users when to use which shortcut. ThinDirect, discussed later in this chapter, in the *Virtualizing Internet Explorer 6* section, will allow you to automatically point the user to the right browser. There are many use cases for launching something natively within a virtualized environment. You may face troublesome Excel add-ons. Virtualizing them will protect against conflicts, but you must launch native Excel within the environment of the add-on for it to work. Here you could use the fact that many Excel add-ons use `.xla` files as the typical entry point to the add-on. Create your entry point using the `.xla` file as source and you will be able to launch any Excel version that is natively installed. When you use a non executable as your entry point source, remember that the name of your entry point must still be `.exe`. The following is an example of an entry point using a text file as source:

```
[ReadMe.exe]
Source=%Drive_C%\Temp\readme.txt
ReadOnlyData=Package.ro.tvr
```

Running `ReadMe.exe` will launch whatever is associated to handle `.txt` files. The application will run within the virtualized environment of the package.

The project folder

The project folder is where the packager spends most of his or her time. The capturing process is just a means to create the project folder. You could just as easily create your own project folder from scratch. I admit, to manually create a project folder representing a Microsoft Office installation would be far from easy but in theory it can be done. There is some default content in all project folders. Let's capture nothing and investigate what these are.

During **Setup Capture**, to speed things up, disable the majority of the search locations. This way pre and post scans will take close to no time at all.

1. Run **Setup Capture**.

2. In the **Ready to Prescan** step, click on **Advanced Scan Locations....**

3. Exclude all but one location from the scanning, as shown in the following screenshot:

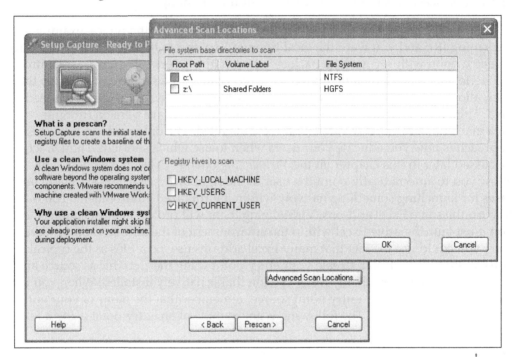

Since we want to capture nothing, there is no point in scanning all locations. Normally you don't have to modify the advanced scan locations.

4. After pressing **Prescan**, wait for **Postscan** to become available and click on it when possible, without modifying anything in your capturing environment.

5. Accept **CMD.EXE** as your entry point and accept all defaults throughout the wizard.

Your project folder will look like the following screenshot:

The project folder of a capturing, bearing no changes, will still create folder macros and default isolation modes.

Let's explore the defaults prepopulated by the **Setup Capture** wizard. This is the minimum project folder content that the **Setup Capture** will ever generate. As a packager you are expected to clean up unnecessary folders from the project folder, so your final project folder may very well contain a smaller number of folder macros. **Folder macros** are ThinApp's variables. `%ProgramFilesDir%` will be translated to `C:\Program Files` on an English Windows installation but the same package running on a Swedish OS the `%ProgramFilesDir%` will point to `C:\Program`. Folder macros are the key to ThinApp packages' portability.

If we explore the filesystem part of the project folder, we'll see the default isolation modes prepopulated by **Setup Capture**. These are applied as defaults no matter what default filesystem isolation mode you choose during the **Setup Capture** wizard. This confuses some people. I'm often told that a certain package is using WriteCopy or Merged as the isolation mode. Well that's just the default used when no other isolation mode is specified. A proper project folder should have isolation modes specified on all locations of importance, basically making the default isolation mode of no importance. The prepopulated isolation modes are there to make sure most applications run out of the box ThinApped. You are expected to change these to suit your application and environment.

Let's look at some examples of default isolation modes.

- `%AppData%`, the location where most applications store user settings, is by default using WriteCopy. This is to make sure that you sandbox all user settings.
- `%SystemRoot%` and `%SystemSystem%` have WriteCopy as their default isolation modes, allowing a virtualized application to see the operating system files without allowing it to modify `C:\Windows` and `C:\Windows\System32`.
- `%SystemSystem%\spool` representing `C:\Windows\System32\Spool` has Merged as its default. This way print jobs will be spooled to the native location, allowing the printer to pick up the print job.
- `%Desktop%` (user's desktop folder) and `%Personal%` (user's document folder) have Merged by default.

When ThinApp generates the project folder, it uses the following logic to decide which isolation mode to prepopulate other locations with. The same logic is used within the registry as well.

- Modified locations will get WriteCopy as the isolation mode
- New locations will get Full as their isolation mode

The Package.ini file

Package.ini, found in the root of the project folder, is the project wide settings file. Here you can apply configuration changes that will be applied to the whole project. Many parameters are prepopulated in `Package.ini`. Some are default ThinApp values and some are from your choices made during **Setup Capture**. I prefer to change very few of the defaults in **Setup Capture**. I'd rather change my project settings within the `Package.ini` file directly. There are quite a few `Package.ini` parameters you can use, though not all of them are listed in `Package.ini` by default. I will explain the parameters that are included by default. A complete list of `Package.ini` parameters are found in *References* of this book. `Package.ini` is structured in different sections. `[BuildOptions]` is the section where you'll find most of the parameters. This section's parameters will be applied project wide, that is, to all of your entry points within the project. `[FileList]`, `[Compression]`, and `[Isolation]` parameters act as the ones under `[BuildOptions]` but are in different sections for backward compatibility reasons. You must place a parameter in its correct section. Luckily, a clear majority of the parameters will live under `[BuildOptions]`. Then you have entry point-specific sections, `[EntryPointName.exe]`. These sections' parameters are only applied to that particular entry point. Only a very few parameters can be used both in `[BuildOptions]` and under `[EntryPointName.exe]`. Most default parameters are commented out in the `Package.ini` file. You can activate the parameter simply by deleting the semicolon in front of the parameter, saving your `Package.ini` file, and rebuilding your project.

Let's have a look at the `Package.ini` file in our `Mozilla Firefox` project folder. Some parts of the file I will cover later in this book. MSI parameters are discussed in the section *Using MSI to distribute packages* in *Chapter 3, Deployment of ThinApp Packages* and AppSync is covered in the section *Application Sync (AppSync)* in *Chapter 5, How to Distribute Updates*.

```
[Compression]
CompressionType=None
```

> `CompressionType` must be located under `[Compression]`. It supports two values, `None` or `Fast`. The `None` value offers no compression of the files within your package. `Fast` will, since Version 4.5 of ThinApp, by default only compress non executables and DLLs. For performance reasons, ThinApp will leave executables and DLLs uncompressed. You can change this behavior using `OptimizeFor=Disk`.

```
[Isolation]
DirectoryIsolationMode=WriteCopy
```

> `DirectoryIsolationMode` specifies the isolation mode used on the filesystem if no other isolation mode has been specified for that particular location.

```
[BuildOptions]
```

> This indicates the start of the build options section.

```
AccessDeniedMsg=You are not currently authorized to run this
application. Please contact your administrator.
```

> This is the message displayed to the user if they try to run a ThinApp package using Active Directory group membership for protection, and the user is not a member of the correct group. It works together with the `PermittedGroups` parameter.

```
CapturedUsingVersion=4.7.1-677178
```

> This identifies which version of ThinApp was used to capture this project.

```
OutDir=bin
```

> This is where the output of your build process will be.

```
SandboxName=Mozilla Firefox (3.5.2)
```

> This is the name of the sandbox used. All entry points within a project share the same sandbox. They are all running within the same virtual environment. Each project must have their own sandbox. You should have one sandbox per user and package. You cannot have two active users or packages sharing the same sandbox. The sandbox will be locked by the first user/package launched.

```
InventoryName=Mozilla Firefox (3.5.2)
```

This is the name of the package. It will be displayed in numerous locations, for example, in Add and Remove programs. It will be picked up by inventory tools and is used to prepopulate the `Package.ini` parameters using the name of the package, for example, `SandboxName` and `MSIFilename`.

```
InventoryIcon=%ProgramFilesDir%\Mozilla Firefox\firefox.exe,0
```

This specifies which icon will be displayed in the application store of **VMware Horizon Application Manager**.

```
;PermittedGroups=Administrators;Remote Desktop Users
```

This is used to lock down the package so that only members of listed Active Directory groups are allowed to execute the entry points of this project. You can use `PermittedGroups` on a per entry point basis as well. The machine where you run `build.bat` must be a domain member in order to pull the **Security Identifier (SID)** of the group. The package will contain the SID of the groups, so when executing it on clients no query will go to the domain controllers, but the locally cached credentials will be used to authorize the user. Instead of entering a group name you can provide the SID of the group. This allows you to build on a machine not being a member of the domain. Using SIDs allows for a package to support multiple domains with no trusts between the domains. This parameter works together with the `AccessDeniedMsg` parameter.

```
;RemoveSandboxOnExit=1
```

This activates the possibility for your package to delete the sandbox when the user shuts down the application.

```
;RemoveSandboxOnStart=1
```

This allows you to delete the sandbox on each launch of an application.

```
;SandboxNetworkDrives=1
```

```
;SandboxRemovableDisk=1
```

By default, removable disks and network drives are not sandboxed. Activate it to change the behavior.

```
;VirtualizeExternalOutOfProcessCOM=0
```

By default, child processes are loaded within the virtual environment of the package calling the child process. There are different methods of calling another process. One is to use COM. `VirtualizeExternalOutOfProcessCOM` specifies if a process called via COM should be loaded within the virtualized environment (default) or not. This parameter together with `ChildProcessEnvironmentExceptions` is often used in order to support integration between virtualized application and natively installed applications.

```
;OptionalAppLinks=plugins\*.exe
;RequiredAppLinks=\\server\share\*.exe;c:\abs\path\file.exe
```

AppLink parameters were discussed in *Chapter 1, Application Virtualization,* in the *Application Linking (AppLink)* section.

```
VirtualDrives=Drive=c, Serial=647c820d, Type=FIXED
;VirtualDrives=Drive=a, Serial=00e20ba8, Type=REMOVABLE; Drive=c,
Serial=647c820d, Type=FIXED; Drive=d, Serial=647c820d, Type=CDROM
```

ThinApp can virtualize drives. By default c: will be active as a virtual drive. This allows ThinApp to present the same c: serial number to the application no matter on which machine the package executes. By default Package.ini is prepopulated with all of the local drives of your capturing environment, but disabled out. Make sure you only have one active VirtualDrives parameter in your Package.ini file. Minimum required values for VirtualDrives are Drive and Type. You do not have to specify a serial number. If you want to virtualize a CD-ROM and add some files on the virtual CD-ROM, you will have to specify the virtual drive in Package.ini first.

```
VirtualDrives=Drive=c, Serial=647c820d, Type=FIXED; Drive=X,
Type=CDROM
```

Then you must create the folder macro (%Drive_X%) representing the virtual drive within your project folder. %Drive_X% is shown in the project folder in the following screenshot:

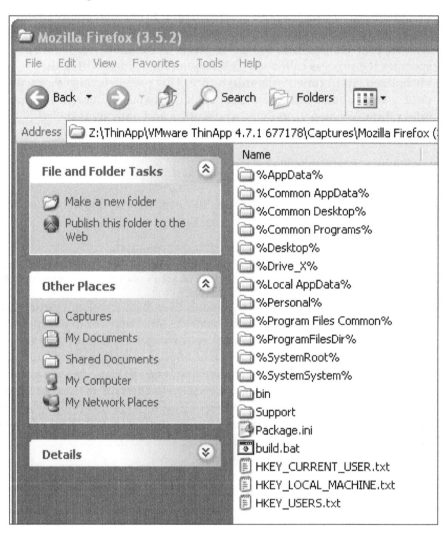

`Drive_X` is the folder macro representing your virtual drive using X: as the drive letter.

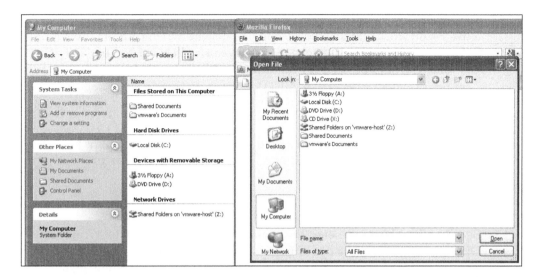

The virtualized X: is only present in the virtualized environment.

`;VirtualComputerName=CNB`

> You can virtualize the computer name within your virtual environment. `Package.ini` will save the computer name from your capturing environment. Some applications will use the computer name and therefore break portability. Another method of allowing portability for such an application is to name your capture machine `LOCALHOST`. This way, all application references to the computer name will use `LOCALHOST`.

`AnsiCodePage=1252`

`LocaleIdentifier=1033`

> You can specify the specific regional settings within the virtual environment. This helps deal with applications changing their behavior depending on which region the operating system has.

`;Wow64=0`

> `Wow64` can sometimes help a 32-bit application to run on a 64-bit operating system. More on capturing on 32-bit and running on a 64-bit OS is available in the *Some packaging tips* section in this chapter.

```
;LoadDotNetFromSystem=Win7
```

If you captured the .NET Framework on a Windows XP machine, you can, by activating this parameter, tell the ThinApp runtime to discard the virtualized .NET Framework and use the system one instead when running on Windows 7. This would allow your package to contain an older version of .NET. The old version would be used on Windows XP but not on Windows 7 (Windows 7 cannot use older versions of .NET).

```
QualityReportingEnabled=1
```

This parameter allows the package to report successful executions to a VMware server for quality assurance. You can disable this feature with the value 0.

```
;IgnoreDDEMessages=1
```

By activating this parameter, the packaged application will not receive any DDE messages from the operating system. This can help you run multiple instances of the same application.Often DDE is used to keep new instances of already loaded applications from loading. This is to preserve memory on the clients. But DDE is often a bad thing if you want to run multiple versions of an application, for example, one instance of Excel Version 2003 and at the same time Excel 2007.

```
;-------- Horizon Parameters ----------
```

```
;AppID=genid
```

```
;NotificationDLLs=HorizonPlugin.dll
```

These two parameters will enable the **VMware Horizon Application Manager** management of the package. Add these two parameters to enable Horizon management in projects captured using old versions of ThinApp. Learn more on Horizon management of ThinApps later in this book.

```
[EntryPointName.exe] or [DataContainerName.dat]
```

This indicates the start of the entry point section. Entry points were discussed earlier in this chapter in the *Entry points and the data container* section.

Isolation mode considerations

You can change isolation modes for folders by modifying the `##Attributes.ini` file within it. This is shown in the following screenshot:

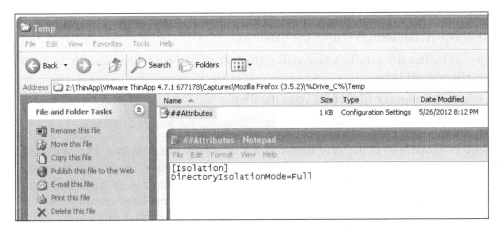

If the folder within your project folder does not contain a `##Attributes.ini` file, simply create one using Notepad or copy one from another folder.

You can change isolation modes on a per-registry sub tree basis using the `isolation_merged`, `isolation_writecopy`, or `isolation_full` parameter in front of the registry location, as shown in the following screenshot:

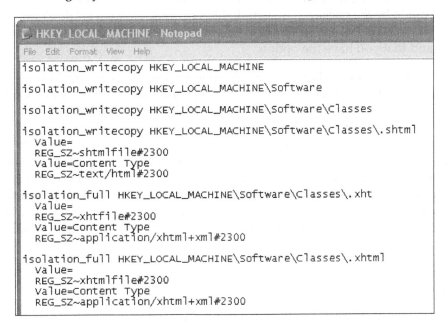

When you package an application it is important to find out which isolation modes are required within the project to get the behavior you want from your package. A packager must test run the package and explore the sandbox. This allows the packager to get to know the application and to know how it behaves as a ThinApp package. Typical things of interest are as follows:

- The initial launch size of the sandbox
- Whether the sandbox size will grow by using the package and by launching it several times
- No temporary files bloat your sandbox
- You can delete the sandbox after exiting the package

A good practice is to make sure the sandbox is as small as possible. This will make the sandbox easier to roam if you are using roaming profiles. In general, there is never any reason to allow the sandbox to grow beyond control. A good ThinApp package, from my point of view, is the smallest possible package creating the smallest possible sandbox. Some applications open files with editing ability without really needing to. If these files are located within the virtual environment, they will end up in the sandbox. There is not much you can do about this. But sometimes you can create a mix between the physical elements (registry and filesystem objects) and virtual elements. For example, you can choose not to sandbox user settings by Using the Merged isolation mode on `%AppData%` and all its subfolders. The benefit of doing this is that your sandbox will be smaller and you can more easily manipulate the settings accessing the native location. The downside is of course that not all changes made by the package are included in one portable folder. I don't prefer one model over another, as both offer their pros and cons. The most important thing is to understand that you have the option.

A question I often get is whether an application packaged using ThinApp supports **Group Policy Objects (GPO)** or not. The answer is simple, both yes and no. GPOs are simply registry keys. You know by now that ThinApp is able to virtualize registry keys and is able to fully isolate native keys. By capturing on a non-domain member, ThinApp will by default create a package that will allow GPOs to be applied to the virtualized application. If you capture on a domain member, you risk capturing some parts of the registry where GPOs are located. Then your package will have fixed GPO settings, that is, when changing your network GPO settings, the package will not see those changes. You can decide to fully isolate the GPO part of the registry so that no GPO settings will be available to the virtualized application.

The following is a list of the isolation mode settings needed to make a ThinApp package unaffected by GPO (by default the virtualized application will honor GPO settings).

- `HKEY_CURRENT_USER.txt`

  `isolation_full HKEY_CURRENT_USER\Software\Policies`

  `isolation_full HKEY_CURRENT_USER\Software\Microsoft\Windows\CurrentVersion\Policies`

- `HKEY_LOCAL_MACHINE.txt`

  `isolation_full HKEY_LOCAL_MACHINE\Software\Policies`

  `isolation_full HKEY_LOCAL_MACHINE\Software\Microsoft\Windows\CurrentVersion\Policies`

Another important thing to consider, when packaging an application, is its integration with other applications, especially locally installed applications. Let's say you virtualize Internet Explorer (IE). Using the package IE, you click on a Word document hosted on a web page. That document will be downloaded into **Temporary Internet Files**. When downloaded, IE will contact `Winword.exe` and request it to open the file that just got downloaded. The folder in this example is what I call a **hand-over-folder**. Hand-over-folder is not a generally used term. I've made it up myself. But it explains quite well what the folder is used for. The hand-over-folder is of greatest importance when it comes to interaction between virtual applications and natively installed ones. It can also be of importance when two virtualized applications, not having been AppLinked, need to interact as well.

If the hand-over-folder is using the WriteCopy or Full isolation mode, then the download in our Internet Explorer example will be sandboxed. Internet Explorer only knows about the normal path to **Temporary Internet Files**, that is, `C:\Documents and Settings\User\Local Settings\Temporary Internet Files`. Virtualized IE has no idea that the correct physical location of the hand-over-folder is actually `C:\Documents and Settings\UserName\Application Data\Thinstall\Internet Explorer\%Internet Cache%`. When Internet Explorer passes over the path to `Winword.exe`, it will be the wrong path. `Winword.exe` will execute and try to access the file, but in vain. It cannot find the file and you are left with an error message stating the file cannot be accessed. The workaround is to make sure that all hand-over-folders are using Merged as their isolation mode. That is to say, go to the hand-over-folder inside the project folder and change the isolation mode in the `##Atributes.ini` file to Merged.

Virtualizing Internet Explorer 6

ThinApp can virtualize any version of Internet Explorer. Virtualizing Internet Explorer 6 (IE6) is a common use case for many companies. If you must migrate to Internet Explorer 8 or you are about to migrate to Windows 7, virtualizing IE6 allows you to continue supporting your legacy web applications. Being able to run multiple versions of IE is a huge benefit. Most versions of Internet Explorer can be installed on Windows XP or Windows 7, and are therefore captured using the normal capturing process of ThinApp. Internet Explorer 6 cannot be captured using the normal process. You could install and capture it on Windows 2000, but that version of IE6 is very different from the one offered on Windows XP. In order to support virtualizing the Windows XP version of Internet Explorer 6, **Setup Capture** has a template describing necessary registry keys and files. You can capture Internet Explorer 6 by starting your Windows XP virtual machine, patching it to the level of Internet Explorer 6 wanted, and then launching **Setup Capture**. Straight after the prescan, before running the postscan, you'll find a button called **Internet Explorer....**

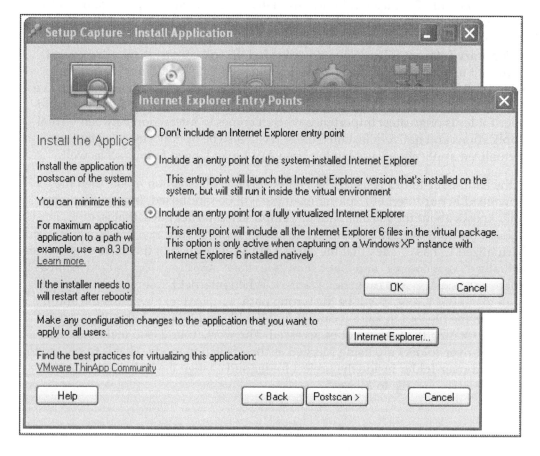

The third option, **Include an entry point for a fully virtualized Internet Explorer**, is only available when running **Setup Capture** on Windows XP with Internet Explorer 6 installed. Choosing the third option will harvest IE6 from the operating system, creating a project folder containing everything needed to virtualize IE6. Since **Setup Capture** is still doing its normal snapshotting you can install Java, Flash, or other components that you want to include in your Internet Explorer 6 package. Internet Explorer 6 packaged with ThinApp runs perfectly on Windows 7. The second option, **Include an entry point for the system-installed Internet Explorer**, will simply create an entry point using the native Internet Explorer as source. This option is very handy when capturing a specific runtime of, for example, Java. Launching the native Internet Explorer within the package will save you from packaging Internet Explorer, saving you from having to maintain and patch two Internet Explorer instances.

Being able to virtualize many variations and versions of browsers is a very powerful feature of ThinApp. But how can we tell the end users which browser to launch for which web application? Your answer is **ThinDirect**. ThinDirect is a browser helper you add to your local Internet Explorer instance. ThinDirect will monitor URLs accessed by the user and automatically redirect the user to the correct browser. ThinDirect supports redirecting to any virtualized browser, such as Chrome, Mozilla Firefox, Safari, and many more, from Internet Explorer. If you redirect to another Internet Explorer instance, ThinDirect's logic is still active so you can force the users to only be able to access certain URLs within a packaged Internet Explorer. When the user tries to access a URL not handled by the package, the user will be redirected back to the native browser.

There are two main methods of deploying the ThinDirect functionality. They are as follows:

- Centrally deploying `ThinDirect.msi` and managing it by using GPO
- Deploying by using the MSI wrapped package, managed with local configuration files

Nothing stops you from using `ThinDirect.msi` with local configuration files or vice versa. If your project folder contains a `ThinDirect.txt` file, then the ThinApp build process will automatically include ThinDirect in the MSI it generates. This means that the ThinDirect browser helper is installed during the deployment of the ThinApp package. The format of the `ThinDirect.txt` files is very straightforward. You specify the entry point and the URL filter you want to ThinDirect.

```
[VirtIE6.exe]
www.saveie6.com
```

When deploying the package, the `ThinDirect.txt` file will get copied onto the machine and its name will be changed to the entry point name. The value between `[]` will be replaced with the path to the entry point. Keep in mind that the ThinDirect browser helper has to be installed machine-wide, that is, installed by a user having local admin privileges.

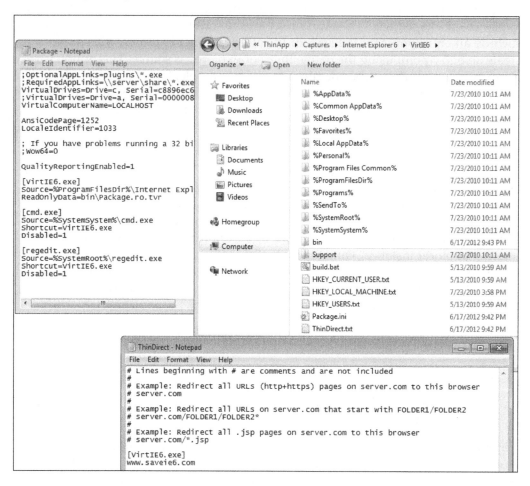

The previous screenshot shows a project folder with ThinDirect activated. `ThinDirect.txt` is not needed when using GPO to manage ThinDirect.

You can turn off the virtual Internet Explorer package, redirecting back to the native browser, by adding the following `Package.ini` parameter.

```
[BuildOptions]
ThinDirectWhitelistOnly=0
```

The ThinDirect URL filter supports wildcards. You can specify the filter in either the blacklist or whitelist format, that is, redirect everything but this specific URL.

```
[VirtIE6.exe]
www.saveie6.com
www.google.com
```

The previous example redirects the URLs `www.saveie6.com` and `www.google.com` to the packaged browser's entry point named `VirtIE6.exe`.

```
[VirtIE6.exe]
https://
```

The previous example redirects all URLs using the HTTPS protocol.

```
[VirtIE6.exe]
-www.saveie6.com
*
```

The previous example redirects everything but `www.saveie6.com`, which will be handled by the native browser.

The recommended ThinApp capture process

The most important thing to understand about your packaging process is that it is a well-defined process that helps you package many applications successfully. Your process may vary but I want to share mine for your reference.

1. Use virtual machines and virtual machine snapshots to keep a repository of the various environments. Choose the environment suitable for the package you want to create. Remember that the starting point will dictate the outcome of your packaging process.

2. Launch the application before running the postscan snapshot. You must make sure the application works as expected and you should customize it to fit your environment. Many applications make a lot of changes to the system on first launch, which are often important to capture. If the application registers its license to the machine in the during its first launch, then you should of course not launch it.

3. I always use WriteCopy as my default filesystem isolation mode. This way I know that I will sandbox everything that the application is modifying. I never activate MSI or compression. At this point they only slow down my build process.

4. Allow **Setup Capture** to build your project and while the application is still natively installed, launch your newly compiled package. Most executions, where the application is locally installed, succeed. If it fails, it is most likely due to one of the two things. Either something is wrong with your entry point or the ThinApp runtime cannot handle the application. If you suspect it's the runtime, then there is not much you can do. There might be workarounds available, for example, loading components outside the virtual environment, but it is not very likely. The best thing to do is to have VMware support have a look at it.

5. Shut down the application and investigate the sandbox. Make sure that the sandbox is as small as possible. Try deleting the sandbox. If denied, there is something keeping the virtual environment from cleanly shutting down. Investigate what it is and make sure the package cleanly shuts down when the user exits the main application.

6. Copy the project folder and package to a network share.

7. Test run on a clean machine. Use the application to the best of your ability. Most of the times you are not a user of the application, but you can hopefully create something, save it, print it, start the built-in help, and try to open something.

8. If everything looks good, create a copy of your project folder and start to clean up the project folder. A good package is as small as possible. Get rid of the installer cache, temp files, and whatever else you can find. If you get a little carried away, you can always revert to your backup copy.

9. Create the production version, changing the default isolation mode if needed, and activate MSI if that's the method used for deployment.

10. Ask the application owner to test run the application before sending it through to the **User Acceptance Test (UAT)**. I prefer to have my project folder on a separate share and copy the package to a separate UAT share for testing, by someone other than me. Make sure no one can tamper with the project folder.

11. If I must change something in the package, I will always make a copy of my project folder and give it a new version number. This way I can always revert my changes. I tend to always change the sandbox name to include my package version. This way I'm guaranteed that a new and fresh sandbox is used. The versioning is shown in the following screenshot:

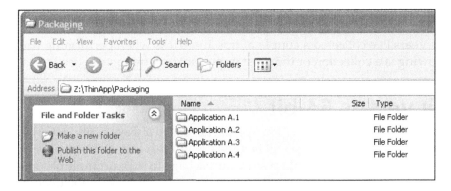

It's important to keep different versions of your project folders. You can delete old versions when you have verified the functionality of the new version, and you know you do not need to revert to an older version.

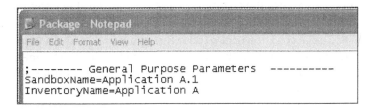

The previous screenshot shows the `Package.ini` file from the first version of the package.

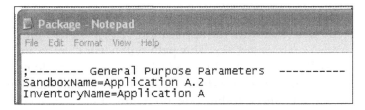

My second version of the package uses a different sandbox name. Changing the sandbox name to reflect your project folder version guarantees that no old settings from the previous test runs will conflict with your changes.

12. During each step of my packaging process I document the process. Each new version gets documented based on what changes are made and why.

Some packaging tips

Over the years I've collected a couple of tips and tricks when performing packaging. The following is a collection of the most important and frequently used ones.

32-bit versus 64-bit

The easiest method of creating a ThinApp package is to always capture it on the same operating system as the package will be used on. But this is not always possible. There are many reasons why you would want your package to support multiple operating systems, and in those cases you must capture it on the lowest common denominator. A 32-bit application captured on a 32-bit operating system, running in a 64-bit environment, is a special kind of beast. The most common reason for trouble is the fact that the Program Files folder change names. When a 32-bit application refers to %ProgramFiles%, the OS will provide C:\Program Files (x86) as the path. But still a 32-bit application can access the C:\Program Files folder. Let's say the application uses XML files and .ini files for configuration. These files may include a path similar to C:\Program Files\ApplicationFolder\MyImportant.dll. In your project folder, the application folder is located in %ProgramFilesDir%\ApplicationFolder. When executing the package on a 64-bit environment, the application folder will therefore be presented as located in C:\Program Files (x86)\ApplicationFolder. This is all well except for the hardcoded XML and .ini files. They still point to C:\Program Files, which will be the 64-bit version of Program Files, and there the application will not find its required components. You have similar behavior within the registry. Sometimes, activating the Wow64 parameter in Package.ini will help you. But far from every time.

A much safer method is to capture the application being installed into a static path, for example, C:\ApplicationFolder. This path will never change and therefore most applications will run on both 32-bit and 64-bit operating systems. When working with 64 bit, make sure no 16-bit code is used by the application. A 64-bit operating system cannot handle 16-bit code, no matter if it's packaged with ThinApp or not. If you can successfully install the application on a 64-bit OS, try capturing it on a 64-bit OS. If you still need one package supporting both 32-bit and 64-bit environments, compare the project folder from a 32-bit OS with the one captured on a 64-bit OS. This should help you to identify differences and hopefully be able to merge it all into one single package. A VBScript can be used to alter registry keys or static configuration files depending on which OS the package runs on. Learn more on VBScript later in this chapter.

Services

If you capture an application installing a service, make sure you shut down the service before running the post-installation snapshot. This way you are guaranteed that the service doesn't lock files keeping the capturing process from accessing them.

Auto update

You should make sure to disable all the applications' built-in auto update functionality. Auto update often runs in the background keeping the virtual environment running even though the user shuts down the main application. If an update is downloaded, it is downloaded and applied into the sandbox. This will bloat the sandbox. As a packager you should be in charge of which version is in production and when. This should not be an auto update feature.

Save your project folders

Always save your project folders! You will always find a reason to return to your old project folders and change some things in order to create a new version of a package. And as Murphy's law dictates, if you capture the application from scratch and follow all your detailed documentation, you will end up with a broken package. I store all my project folders on a network share that is protected by a backup. You could zip the old project folders to preserve space.

Make sure you investigate the sandbox

When the application is captured and installed, I always run my newly built package. This way I can very quickly investigate the sandbox and see if something is bloating it. I can then try and delete the sandbox contents. If this doesn't work, something is keeping the virtual environment from shutting down cleanly. This should be dealt with. Using **Process Explorer** from *Sysinternals*, available at `http://technet.microsoft.com/en-US/sysinternals`, is probably the easiest method to find out what is keeping the sandbox locked. Simply run the Process Explorer and search for `.RW`. `.RW` is part of the registry filenames and is always in use by the process keeping the virtual environment open.

When capturing, make sure you are capturing!

This means that on your capturing machine, while performing the capturing process, you shouldn't use the environment to browse to Facebook.com or download a cool tool you will try out later. Everything you do on the machine will pollute your project folder. It may be boring to look at the installation wizard and not do anything, but that is the only way to make sure nothing goes wrong. Some error messages may flash by.

Make sure your application is 100 percent natively installed

You cannot expect your ThinApp package to run perfectly if the native installation doesn't run perfectly. Before you start to troubleshoot your package, verify the full functionality of the installation you captured. Troubleshooting a ThinApp package created on a machine where the native installation wasn't running is a guaranteed waste of time. It will be close to impossible to fix it.

Never start with AppLink

If you plan to create a package using AppLink, capture everything in one big package first. This way you can verify the functionality and integration first. If there are any issues, it's much easier to troubleshoot one single package than multiple packages using AppLink.

VB Scripting

When deploying an application using legacy methods, it is possible to customize the application upon installation. This is not possible with a ThinApp package because you can never actually install the application. You can simply execute the application. So for ThinApp to support customization of a package, there is a VBScript engine built into the runtime. Using VB Scripting built into your packages offers great flexibility. Virtually anything can be scripted. The VBScript can interact with both the virtual and the physical environment. Many times VBScripts are used to change the package upon launch, for example, reading the version of the operating system that the package is currently executing on, and changing the package content.

Many customers use VBScript for protection. If you do not have an Active Directory you can create your own logic as a VBScript file and if not fulfilled, this shuts down the package. You can add the VBScript functionality simply by copying your script into the root of your project folder and hitting `build.bat`. The name of your VBScript file can be anything, but it must end with `.vbs`. You can have multiple scripts in the root of the project folder, but the execution order will then depend on the name of the scripts. It's much better to only have one VBScript present in the root of the project folder. If you want to call on other scripts you can do so from within your main VBScript.

ThinApp supports four different callback functions when the VBScript file gets executed. They are as follows:

- `OnFirstSandboxOwner`

  This is the first thing that happens when a user launches an entry point. Before the source of the entry point is launched, VBScript will execute this code. The `OnFirstSandboxOwner` function runs only once per lock of the sandbox. So if you have packaged a suite of applications, for example, Microsoft Office, the `OnFirstSandboxOwner` function will run when Excel is started, but not when Word is launched if Excel is left running.

- `OnFirstParentStart`

  This function executes every time a parent process is launched. Using the previous example with MS Office, launching Excel will run the code. Launching Word while Excel is still running will launch the code one more time.

- `OnFirstParentExit`

  This code gets executed on every parent process exit. It launches when you shut down Excel and it runs one more time when you exit Word.

- `OnLastProcessExit`

  This is the last thing that happens before the virtual environment is closed down and the sandbox is unlocked. You exit Word, nothing happens, but when you exit Excel the script is called.

Example scripts

```
Function OnFirstSandboxOwner
msgbox "Hello World!"
End Function
```

This script will display **Hello World!** when you launch the first process.

```
Function OnFirstSandboxOwner
msgbox "Hello World!"
End Function
msgbox "Hello again!"
```

This script will display **Hello World!** when the first parent is launched. It will display **Hello again!** for all the parent or child processes launched. If you test run the previous script, you will notice that the part of the script that isn't within a function will execute first. Even before OnFirstSandboxOwner.

ThinApp uses its own built-in script engine. It supports most VBScript commands but not all. WSCRIPT.<commands> is not supported. ThinApp has added the following extra commands since a normal VBScript doesn't understand a virtual environment:

- AddForcedVirtualLoadPath

  This tells the ThinApp runtime to handle all the DLLs in the location as virtual, even when they are not located within the virtual environment.

- ExitProcess

  This will quit the current process. A use case example would be to protect the package from unauthorized usage. That means if something is not fulfilled, run ExitProcess. You can add exit codes if needed.

  Example: ExitProcess 0

  This provides exit code 0, that is, no errors.

- ExpandPath

  ExpandPath tells the ThinApp runtime to expand folder macros. When using VBScript, it is important to realize that system variables and folder macros are not the same. Use ExpandPath to convert a folder macro into a system format.

- ExecuteExternalProcess

  This will run a certain process outside the virtual environment. This will allow you to manipulate the physical environment from your script. Bear in mind that the package, and therefore also the script, executes in the context of the user.

- ExecuteVirtualProcess

  This is the same as ExecuteExternalProcess, but runs within the virtual environment instead.

- GetBuildOption

  This is a command to get the Package.ini file's [BuildOptions] parameters. You can add your own parameters to Package.ini and access them using GetBuildOptions.

- GetFileVersionValue

  This returns the version information about a file.

- GetCommandLine

  This gets the command line parameter that is passed to an application.

- GetCurrentProcessName

  This returns the full virtual path to a process.

- GetOSVersion

  This returns the operating system version.

- GetEnvironmentVariable

  This fetches environment variables into the script.

- RemoveSandboxOnExit

  This will delete the sandbox content upon exit.

- SetEnvironmentVariable

  This specifies a value to an environment variable.

- SetFileSystemIsolation

  Normally, you need to rebuild your project folder if you want to change the isolation mode for a location. Using SetFileSystemIsolation will allow you to specify the isolation mode on the filesystem via a script.

- `SetRegistryIsolation`

  This is the equivalent of `SetFileSystemIsolation` but for the registry.

- `WaitForProcess`

  This waits until a certain process ends. The process can come from either `ExecuteExternalProcess` or `ExecuteVirtualProcess`.

> The ThinApp manual provides more detailed information with example scripts. For the online version, please visit `http://pubs.vmware.com/thinapp4/help/` or download the PDF version found at `http://www.vmware.com/support/pubs/thinapp_pubs.html`. The ThinApp blog contains a lot of VBScript details as well, `http://blogs.vmware.com/thinapp/scripts`.

Packaging applications with dependencies

There are three kinds of application dependencies as I see it:

- Dependencies on runtimes such as Java or Flash
- Dependencies on locally installed applications
- Dependencies on another virtualized application, for example, packaged Internet Explorer integrates with packaged Adobe Reader

Dependencies on runtimes

When it comes to dependencies on runtimes, there are different strategies you can choose for your deployment methods. My favorite, for most of the environments, is having the latest, greatest runtime version locally installed. Most of your applications can use this version and the ThinApp packages can make use of natively installed components.

I tend to package together only the application that requires a really old version of the runtime with its dependencies. Now I have one single self-contained package including both the application and its dependency.

If you have a couple of applications requiring the same special version of a runtime, I would use AppLink. I package all the applications separately and create another package including only the dependency. This way I am free to maintain application packages without having to touch the runtime package.

Any variations of previously mentioned instances are of course just as valid. ThinApp is a smorgasbord of features and is very flexible in its implementation. You should choose whichever method works best in your environment. The goal is to create the easiest possible environment to maintain. Is it easier to maintain a certain component locally? Then by all means, deploy it locally.

If you want to create a package without its dependency, your capturing machine must have the runtime locally installed before running **Setup Capture**. If you plan to AppLink two packages, the easiest method is to run **Setup Capture**, capture the installation of the runtime, and while the runtime is still locally installed run **Setup Capture** again, capturing the application. This way you know that the application was captured using the settings of your runtime package. If you have many applications requiring a certain runtime as AppLink, it's wise to keep a virtual machine snapshot of the installation of your runtime, which you can use when capturing the applications.

Dependencies on locally installed applications

When you want a package to integrate with a natively installed application, there are a couple of things to keep in mind. It all depends on how the native application behaves when called from the virtualized environment. Some applications do not allow multiple instances of themselves loaded at the same time. When already running and called upon again, the process will simply create a new window within the already running process. If this is the case, you must make sure that any hand-over-folders are using the Merged isolation mode. The hand-over-folder is the location used to pass files between applications. If you are not using Merged, the content will be sandboxed and the path, passed from the virtualized application to the native one will be wrong, and will not contain the files. The risk with packaging applications integrated to native ones is inconsistent behavior. If the application is already running, it will be loaded inside the virtual environment when called upon (child processes are by default launched within the virtual environment) and therefore have access to the hand-over-folder irrespective of whether it's sandboxed or not. But if the application is already running, it will fail to find the files if they are being sandboxed. Sometimes the native application will be confused when launched inside the virtual environment and it is common to see MSI's self-repair kick in. A common and effective solution to the problem of integrating with a locally installed application is to make sure that the native application never runs within the virtual environment. There are different ways a process can be called upon. Using COM is one, and its setting, `VirtualizeExternalOutOfProcessCOM`, was discussed in *The Package.ini* file section of this chapter. `ChildProcessEnvironmentExceptions` handles the other method of calling the process and most of the times you will use both together.

```
[BuildOptions]
VirtualizeExternalOutOfProcessCOM=0
ChildProcessEnvironmentExceptions=WINWORD.EXE;EXCEL.EXE
ChildProcessEnvironmentDefault=Virtual
```

This example will always run `Winword.exe` and `Excel.exe` externally from the virtual environment. `ChildProcessEnvironmentDefault=Virtual` is not really needed. The `Virtual` parameter is the default behavior of the ThinApp runtime. I tend to include it in `Package.ini` to make it easier to read.

Dependencies on another virtualized application

If your package has dependencies to other packaged applications, AppLink is the easiest method for integrating them. But sometimes registering the two packages on the machine is enough for the integration to work. With the help of the previous method, keeping a native application external from the virtual environment, you can make sure that you do not run a ThinApp package within another ThinApp package. It usually works, but is not recommended. AppLinking two packages together will allow for 100 percent integration. Both applications see each other as locally installed on the same machine.

Summary

In this chapter you have learned the packaging process. You have also learned about virtualizing Internet Explorer and using ThinDirect. We have discussed the defaults in `Package.ini` and some best packaging practices. The next chapter will discuss how to deploy packages to your end users.

3
Deployment of ThinApp Packages

In this chapter you will learn about the different methods of deploying ThinApp packages. The previous chapter taught you how to create the package. Now we need to get that package to our end users. In this chapter you'll learn about:

- Deploying ThinApp packages using MSI and traditional deployment tools
- How to register packages using streaming
- Using alternative methods for deployment
- Using VMware Horizon Application Manager to manage your ThinApp packages
- How to use VMware View Manager to entitle ThinApps to desktops

Different deployment scenarios

There are many different methods for deploying ThinApp packages. All of these methods can happily coexist and one doesn't rule out another. There are two main methods, local deployment and streaming.

Local deployment means the packages live on the client's hard drive. The users can use the virtualized application without being connected to the corporate network. One obvious benefit is that you will be able to use the application offline and don't have to depend on the network to be up and running. Another benefit is that the performance of your virtual application doesn't depend on the performance of the network. The downside is that you need to be in touch with your clients. You must get those packages copied to your clients. When a new version of the package is available you'll have to deploy the update to all of your clients again.

Streaming means that the packages reside on a network share. The only infrastructure required is a Microsoft Windows file server. You don't have to install and maintain any server component. Your clients can execute the packages over the network, downloading only the needed blocks. The benefits of this method are that you don't need to deploy anything to your clients and that it's a dead simple update mechanism. The downside is that you can't use the application offline. Streaming requires a constant connection to your streaming network share.

One of the greatest ThinApp features is that both methods are supported using the same package. There's no need to create a special version of your package simply because you want to stream it or use a local deployment method. This, combined with the portability of ThinApp packages, offers a truly unique flexibility and ease of management.

Using streaming deployment

Streaming a ThinApp package means the package is hosted on the network and the clients access the packaged application over the network. The application is executed on the local client. So ThinApp streaming is nothing like **Server Based Computing (SBC)** where the word streaming is often being used as well. In SBC, the execution of the application happens on the server backend and only screen updates are sent to the clients. Commonly used Server Based Computing systems include Citrix XenApp and Microsoft Terminal Server/RDS.

When a user clicks on a ThinApp package, the ThinApp runtime is downloaded to the client in whole. The ThinApp runtime is approximately 600 KB so this happens very quickly. When downloaded, the runtime executes and creates the awareness of the virtual environment. It is not like the whole virtual environment is downloaded, but the runtime makes sure it loads the filesystem database and virtual registry. Then the source of the entry point is executed. What happens later is all up to the source executable. Whatever parts are requested by the application will be pulled down over the network. The ThinApp package stores the filesystem in a structured manner and keeps track of the blocks that contain their respective data. This allows for true streaming, only downloading the requested blocks.

Because a Server Based Computing implementation requires considerable infrastructure, it's understandable if you would like to use ThinApp as a replacement. Before you can make the decision to replace your SBC implementation with ThinApp, you must first investigate why Server Based Computing is being used. There are two reasons to use SBC. The first situation that would require a SBC solution is when you have the combination of a poor bandwidth or high latency **wide area network (WAN)** and an application that consumes a lot of bandwidth or requires a low latency connection to backend servers. In this case, ThinApp will not be able to replace your SBC infrastructure. ThinApp Streaming will download the binaries to the local client, executing the application locally and will therefore be faced with the same WAN connection constraints as a locally installed application. In this case, ThinApp can complement your SBC implementation rather than replacing it. Using Server Based Computing together with ThinApp, you will have much less application conflicts and therefore fewer server silos. Not installing applications locally will keep your SBC infrastructure clean, stable, and obviously easier to maintain. Approximately 30 percent of all ThinApp implementations are ThinApp being used to enhance Server Based Computing implementations, most of them being Citrix XenApp implementations.

If the reason for using SBC is that you don't have to deploy applications, then ThinApp is often a very valid option. There are many benefits to executing the application locally rather than executing it centrally on a server. Having local access to all client devices is one big benefit.

The only infrastructure required for ThinApp streaming is a plain old Windows file share. You place your packages on a file share, point your users to the package, and that's it. How to point your users to the package will be discussed in depth in the *Using thinreg.exe to register your applications* section later in this chapter. It is recommended to have at least a 100 Mbit/s **local area network (LAN)** connection to the file share, but I would recommend 1000 Mbit/s. The connection to the file share must be of low latency and reliable. If you lose the connection to the file share, it's similar to losing the hard drive from the application's point of view. No Windows application is written to cope with the loss of the hard drive during execution, so the application will simply crash and burn when it requests more bits to be loaded.

For **high availability (HA)**, Microsoft **Distributed File System** (DFS) is often used. DFS synchronizes the content of a file share between many file servers. This way, your users will still have access to the packages even if one file server is down. Another benefit of using DFS is that the namespace is shared among all servers. This way you can refer to a package (using \\DomainName\dfsroot\PathToPackage) in your login script and the users will always be connected to the closest DFS server.

Users should have read and execute permissions on the network share. Only the administrators should have the permission to modify on the share. You should make sure that the client and server antivirus is disabled for on-access scanning of your packages. If your antivirus scans the package, the whole package will be downloaded over the network and you will lose the block-by-block scanning as a streaming functionality for the ThinApp runtime.

The size of your packages has very little to do with their actual performance while streaming. Since only the requested blocks will be downloaded, a large package doesn't necessarily mean slow performance or startup time. Most modern applications will dynamically load the necessary files in order to present a GUI (that is, Graphical User Interface) to the user and allow him or her to start using the application. A legacy application may require 100 percent of itself in memory before presenting a GUI, but luckily these applications are often quite small in size.

It's difficult to offer reference architecture and best practices when it comes to streaming as there are so many variables to take into account. Packages of the same application can perform in many different ways. Things to look out for are virtualized fonts and services being started upon launch of the package and large files being copied into the sandbox. If possible, activate fonts on the native client rather than virtualizing them. Loading many virtualized fonts can be time consuming and will affect your package's launch time. Services are always a launch time bottleneck. Often you can disable the auto start of services and your application will happily launch and then start the service when needed. You can disable auto start of services with the Package.ini parameter:

```
[BuildOptions]
AutoStartServices=0
```

If large files are copied into the sandbox, it often means the files have to be copied over the network to the sandbox. This will of course slow down performance. It gets even worse if you store the sandbox on a network share as well. Then you are hit by the network's performance twice. Try to clean up your project. When sizing your file servers and network, it's important to benchmark your packages. You need to investigate how much bandwidth is consumed when launching the package, and you must have an idea of how many users might launch the application at the same time. Having 100 packages and 1,000 users doesn't mean all users launch all 100 packages at the same time. Hosting ThinApp packages is just like hosting Excel or Word files for a file server. There is no real difference from a file serving point of view. So whatever sizing logic you use for your Office documents should also be valid here. You can't look at the size of the package or what the virtualized application consumes in memory when launched, since these two variables have no direct impact on streaming performance. A large memory footprint and a large package may indicate that a lot of data is needed to execute the application, and therefore it will consume a lot of bandwidth. That much is true, but streaming performance relies just as much on the actual code of the application and things such as which language it is written in and which compiler is used.

ThinApp Streaming will stream the application into memory only. The Windows operating system might cache its memory to the disk, but besides that ThinApp Streaming will never touch the disk. This is especially important in a **virtual desktop infrastructure (VDI)** environment such as VMware View. When using VDI, application virtualization is more or less a must. You do not want application entitlement to force a change of the user's disk space consumption. A cost efficient VDI implementation uses a Golden Image, a parent disk containing the operating system and common applications all users should have access to. A **linked clone** disk keeps the user's unique data. This user unique disk should be kept as small as possible for you to save money on an expensive **storage area network (SAN)**. Being able to entitle users to applications and streaming these applications into memory means that very little, if anything, will be changed on the user's unique disk.

ThinApp Streaming is often used on Citrix XenApp servers as well. The fact that the servers are kept clean and conflict free is of course appealing. Streaming means you have just one instance of the package serving your whole XenApp infrastructure. Replacing this package will update all your XenApp servers and users. Later in this book, I'll describe how to update a streaming package in full production with no downtime for the users.

Streaming is mostly used in VDI or Citrix XenApp/Terminal services environments. You can very well stream to physical clients such as desktops or laptops, but it's not as common. When it comes to physical clients, local deployment is often the preferred method. The next section will cover local deployment.

Using MSI to distribute packages

When deploying a ThinApp package locally, the most common method is to use the MSI format. That being said, you could very well just copy the package down to the client's hard drive. ThinApp can generate an MSI wrapper around the package. Any deployment tool supporting the MSI format can use the MSI file. You can activate creation of an MSI file by deleting the semicolon in front of the MSIFilename parameter in `Package.ini` and running `build.bat`.

There are two different MSI file formats that you can create. The first alternative is a self-contained MSI file, containing both the MSI logic and the actual package files (entry points and the data container). The second alternative keeps the package files outside the MSI file. If you choose to have the package files outside the MSI file, the MSI file and the package files must all be located in the same folder. MSIStreaming is the parameter defining which MSI format you'll compile. MSIStreaming=0 will create a self-contained MSI file and MSIStreaming=1 will keep the package files externally from the MSI file.

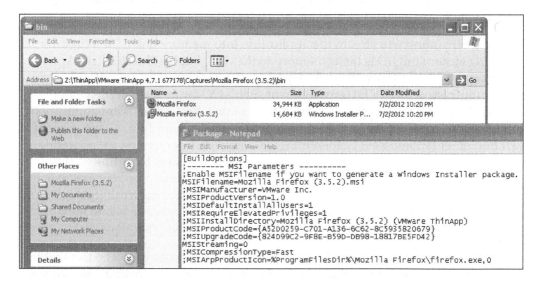

Using MSIStreaming=0 creates an MSI file containing the package file. The package is always created whether you activated MSI or not. Note the differences in size between the original package file and the MSI file. By default the content of the MSI file is compressed.

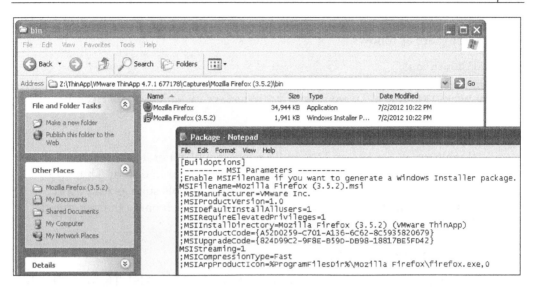

Using `MSIStreaming=1` will not include the package files in the MSI and therefore the MSI files are much smaller.

A ThinApp MSI file built using `MSIStreaming=0` does not have the file size limitation of 2 GB that traditional MSI files have. ThinApp developers have found a clever way to store much more data in an MSI file while maintaining compatibility with all existing deployment tools. This is mentioned in the following blog post: `http://blogs.vmware.com/thinapp/2010/03/vmware-thinapp-45-whats-new.html`. Ever since this special method of storing content within the MSI file was implemented, it's not been possible to edit the MSI generated by ThinApp. If you do, the file will become corrupted. In order to be able to customize the MSI file, you need to apply your changes to the `template.msi` file found in the ThinApp utilities folder. (`template.msi` is used when compiling your MSI file) or use MSIStreaming=1.

The MSI file that ThinApp generates will copy the package to your clients' hard drives. The MSI file also includes the ThinApp tool called **thinreg.exe**. `thinreg.exe` is used to register the package to provide the look and feel of a locally installed application. `thinreg.exe` is launched as a custom action. `thinreg.exe` is such an important tool that I have a whole section focusing on it later in this chapter.

There are quite a few `Package.ini` parameters related to MSI. The defaults found in `Package.ini` are as follows:

```
[BuildOptions]
;-------- MSI Parameters ----------
;EnableMSIFilename if you want to generate a Windows Installer
package.
;MSIFilename=Mozilla Firefox (3.5.2).msi
```

Enable `MSIFilename` and the build process will generate an MSI file containing your package. The MSI file is often used to deploy ThinApp packages with the help of existing deployment tools such as Microsoft SCCM or similar. The parameter also decides which name the generated MSI will have.

```
;MSIManufacturer=VMware Inc.
```

This specifies the manufacturer property within your MSI. The default value is the company name your capture machines' Windows is registered to.

```
;MSIProductVersion=1.0
```

`MSIProductVersion` is used to identify versions of your packages deployed via MSI. If you create a new version and activate this parameter with a higher value, the new MSI will be able to update existing deployments of the package.

```
;MSIDefaultInstallAllUsers=1
```

This specifies if the MSI should be deployed on a machine-wide basis, for all users, or on a per user basis. `MSIDefaultInstallAllUsers=1` will deploy the package machine wide, with the `Program Files` folder as the default location. `MSIDefaultInstallAllUsers=0` will deploy per user, with the user's profile as the default location. `MSIDefaultInstallAllUsers=2` will first try to deploy machine wide but if not permitted it will revert to per user basis.

```
;MSIRequireElevatedPrivileges=1
```

This specifies if the MSI file will require elevated privileges or not. By default, you will be prompted with a UAC prompt on systems supporting UAC.

```
;MSIInstallDirectory=Mozilla Firefox (3.5.2) (VMware ThinApp)
```

This specifies the name of the folder created during deployment and where the package will be placed.

```
;MSIProductCode={A52D0259-C701-A136-6C62-8C5935820679}
```

Globally unique identifier (GUID) is used to identify the package. ThinApp will handle the creation of the product code automatically and most of the times you can leave this parameter commented out.

```
;MSIUpgradeCode={824D99C2-9F8E-B59D-DB98-18817BE5FD42}
```

GUID which is used to identify the package to facilitate version control. Using `MSIProductCode` together with `MSIUpgradeCode` allows updating an existing package with a newer version. ThinApp handles upgrade code automatically and you normally leave this parameter commented out.

```
;MSIStreaming=0
```

This specifies if ThinApp should include the package files (entry points and the data container) in the MSI file or leave them external. ThinApp supports MSI files larger than 2 GB, so normally you can keep all files within the MSI. If you are using VMware View and View Manager to entitle ThinApp packages to virtual desktops, you can use `MSIStreaming=1`. This will allow you to choose within the View Manager if the package should be streamed or be locally deployed to your virtual desktops. If you use the default value of `MSIStreaming=0`, you can only choose to deploy the packages locally. When using `MSIStreaming=1` you must keep the MSI file, entry points, and the data container together in the same folder.

```
;MSICompressionType=Fast
```

This is used to define whether you want to compress the contents of your MSI file or not. Available parameters are `None` or `Fast`.

```
;MSIArpProductIcon=%ProgramFilesDir%\Mozilla Firefox\firefox.exe,0
```

This specifies which icon should be used in **Add or Remove Programs** in the **Control Panel** window. The parameter supports an index of icons within a file.

Using VMware Horizon Application Manager

VMware Horizon Application Manager is a universal services broker and workspace. From Version 1.5, Horizon can entitle users to both **SaaS** (that is, **Software as a Service**) based applications and ThinApp packages. Horizon supports a user-based entitlement system with device and location awareness. This means you can entitle users to applications but with policies you can define when, from where, and on which device an application can be used. Horizon Application Manager has an agent you can deploy to all your Windows-based clients. With the help of this agent, Horizon can deploy ThinApp packages. It is the Horizon Agent that verifies whether you are entitled, based on policies, to run a certain application. Horizon Agent Version 1.5 supports both streaming and local deployment of ThinApp packages. You can specify which mode the agent should use during installation.

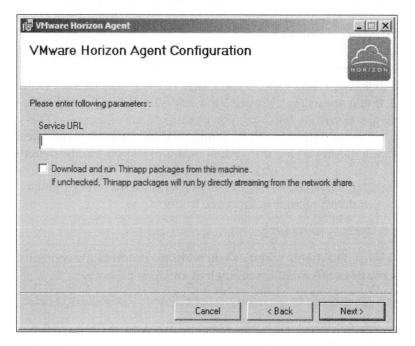

During the installation of Horizon Agent you can decide if ThinApp packages should be downloaded locally or streamed from a network share.

In order for Horizon to be able to manage a ThinApp package, the package must include a couple of `Package.ini` parameters, as follows:

```
[BuildOptions]
InventoryIcon=%SystemSystem%\cmd.exe
```

`InventoryIcon` will offer a suite icon if a project includes many entry points. Instead of listing, for example, `Winword.exe` and `Excel.exe` as two separate icons, in the Horizon Administration interface, both the entry points will be grouped together using the icon specified using the InventoryIcon parameter.

```
;-------- Horizon Parameters ----------
AppID=genid
```

The `AppID` parameter tells the ThinApp build process to generate a GUID used by Horizon to identify the package. The Horizon Application Manager uses this GUID rather than the name of the package. This guarantees that the packages are uniquely identified.

```
NotificationDLLs=HorizonPlugin.dll
```

This tells the package that it needs to communicate with the Horizon Agent upon launch. The Horizon Agent verifies the package's policy and communicates back to the ThinApp runtime whether it is allowed to launch or not.

```
HorizonOrgUrl=http://www.test.com
```

This specifies the URL to your Horizon Service Portal. If the end user doesn't have the Horizon Agent locally installed, the user will get a dialog box telling them they need to install the agent. The dialog box presents a link to the `HorizonOrgUrl` parameter to download the agent.

The two parameters that will activate Horizon Management in a ThinApp package are `AppID=genid` and `NotificationDLLs=HorizonPlugin.dll`. If a package is built with these parameters active, the package will not be able to run on a machine that doesn't have the Horizon Agent installed. If the Horizon Agent is installed, the policy must allow the end user to run the package. There are many methods to protect your ThinApp packages from being used by unauthorized persons, for example, Active Directory groups, VBScript, third-party tools such as Concept Software's SoftwareKey available at `http://www.softwarekey.com`, but using Horizon Application Manager is probably the most feature-rich method.

Horizon is supported from Version 4.7 of ThinApp. With Version 4.7.2 of ThinApp is the `relink.exe` tool was enhanced with the `-h` switch. Using `-h` will inject the Horizon `Package.ini` parameters into an existing package without the need to rebuild the project. This is a very quick and convenient method to enable Horizon support in your existing ThinApp packages. If your package has a separate data container, make sure you run `relink.exe` using *.* to update all entry points and the data container at the same time. This will allow for the same AppID GUID to be used for all entry points as well as the data container

Using VMware View

VMware View is VMware's virtual desktop infrastructure product. The use of virtual applications greatly enhances your VDI implementation. Using application virtualization makes management easier and studies have shown much greater return on investment compared to not using application virtualization. An optimal VDI design makes use of floating pools (no user has their own dedicated desktop) and Golden Images. Using a Golden Image means you have one image containing all shared content such as operating system and applications used by all your users. User unique information is stored either in the user's profile or on a user specific linked clone disk. In order to minimize the usage of expensive SAN disk space, the profile is often redirected to a network share using profile management tools. The only variable left is the linked clone. In minimizing the size of the linked clone, application virtualization is your best friend. Application entitlement and usage will not have to alter the disk content.

View has built-in support for ThinApp entitlement. You can entitle packages to pools of desktops or single desktops. In the View Manager you can't entitle on a per-user basis. This is a limitation and one of the reasons many large implementations of the View use `thinreg.exe` and login scripts to handle application entitlements instead.

The View Manager has two supported methods of entitling ThinApp packages: local deployment and streaming. Local deployment will alter the users' unique disk footprint and is therefore not preferred. The only reason I can see the need for using local deployment is if you are going to use offline desktops. The current version of VMware View (Version 5.1) has no logic for pulling down streaming applications when checking out an offline desktop, and will therefore leave you with local deployment as your only alternative for a true offline usage. Streaming is by far the most preferred method in a VDI environment. The View Manager uses ThinApp MSI files to entitle ThinApps. The View Manager depends on information stored in the MSI file generated by ThinApp. So to be able to manage ThinApp packages within the View Manager, you need to generate an MSI file. Using the `MSIStreaming` parameter, you can change the behavior of the MSI file generated. `MSIStreaming=1` creates the package in such a way that the **View Administrator** can choose to entitle users with either streaming or local deployment of packages. If your packages use `MSIStreaming=0`, only local deployment (called **Full deployment** in the View Manager) will be available as an option. This is shown in the following screenshot:

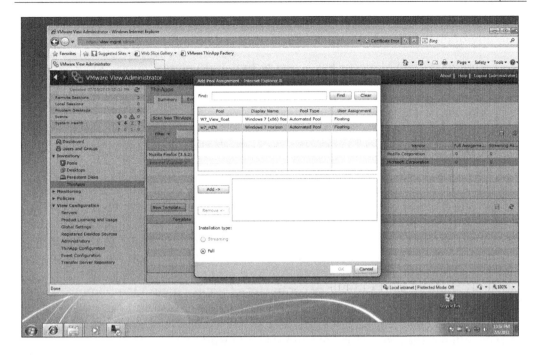

Using `MSIStreaming=0` (package defaults) will only offer you local deployment (**Full**) of packages in the View Manager. The streaming option is grayed out.

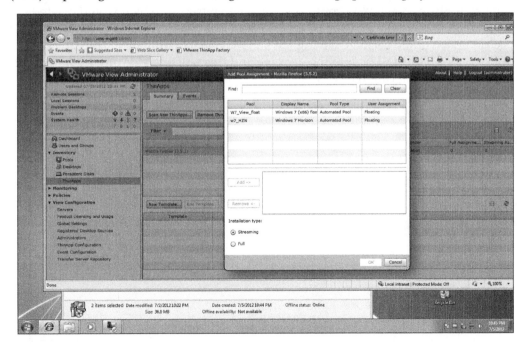

Using `MSIStreaming=1` will give you the possibility of deploying the package either as locally deployed (**Full**) or **Streaming**.

Make sure your View Manager has access to the ThinApp repository. View services must be running with a user account that has at least read access to the repository. ThinApp is bundled with the VMware View Premier license.

Using alternative media and methods

In order to use an application packaged with ThinApp, all you need access to is the package. This gives you unique flexibility. There are many ways to provide access to the package. You can store it on a USB key and give the USB key to your user. You can use **Dropbox** or any other file sharing method to distribute the packages to the end users. I'm not saying you should throw out any existing deployment tool you may have in place. But you should consider using alternative methods if you don't have an effective method of managing applications today. Let's say you have to deploy an application to a couple of contractors. Simply create a Dropbox share, put the application package on the share, invite all the contractors and you're done! No deployment tool agent needs to be installed on the contractors' machines and so you have not altered the contractors' machines in any way.

If you place your package on a USB key, you have your application with you anywhere. It's handy to keep the sandbox on the same USB key so all the settings follow with the package. You could specify `SandboxPath=.`,which would create the sandbox in the same location as the package. But you don't need to maintain a special version of the package having the `SandboxPath=` parameter. You can create a folder called **Thinstall** next to the package and this will override any `Package.ini` settings and be the location of your sandbox.

Creating a folder called **Thinstall** next to the package will override the sandbox location. The previous screenshot shows the sandbox together with the package on a USB key.

Using thinreg.exe to register your applications

`thinreg.exe` is the tool used to register a package in order to give it the look and feel of a locally-installed application. Registering a package will register file types, protocols, and object types, create shortcuts and add the package to **Add or Remove Programs**. You can run any application packaged using ThinApp by simply clicking on an entry point, but running the application will not register the application.

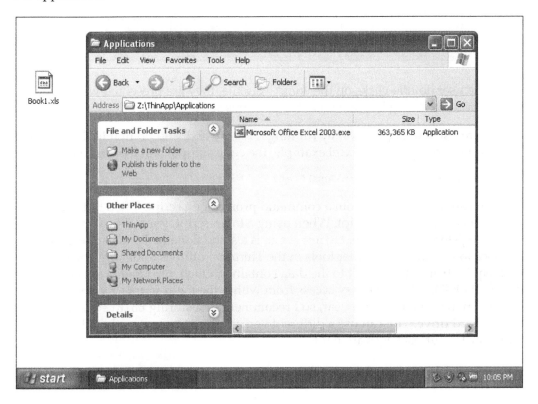

Running Excel packaged with ThinApp does not register the `.xls` file type. The operating system does not know how to handle the Excel file.

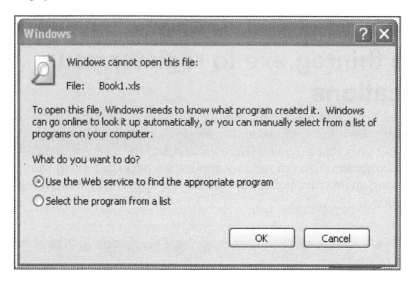

When the user double-clicks on the `Book1.xls` file, they are presented with the not so user-friendly dialog box shown in the previous screenshot.

You can register an application by running `thinreg.exe` and point it to the package. When we use our previous Excel example, the code snippet will look as follows:

```
thinreg.exe "Z:\ThinApp\Applications\Microsoft Office Excel 2003.exe"
```

You can run `thinreg.exe` from a command prompt or a script. Often `thinreg.exe` is called from a login script. When using a login script, your ThinApp packages will be registered upon login. `thinreg.exe` is a standalone tool and can be copied to any location. Many of the other tools in the ThinApp utilities folder are entry points that require being stored next to the data container. Often, `thinreg.exe` is placed in the NETLOGON share for easy access from within the login scripts. `thinreg.exe` is updated two or three times a year, so I recommend not storing `thinreg.exe` on your clients' hard drive. You can use a different version of `thinreg.exe` than the ones with which your packages are built.

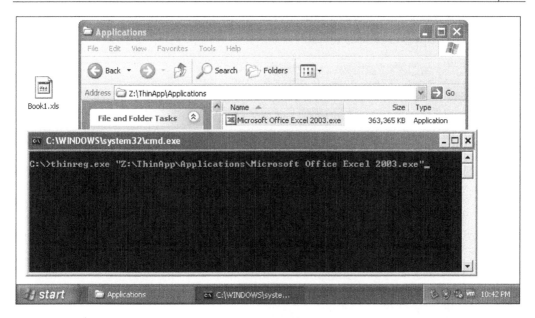

In the previous screenshot, `thinreg.exe` is placed in the root of C:.

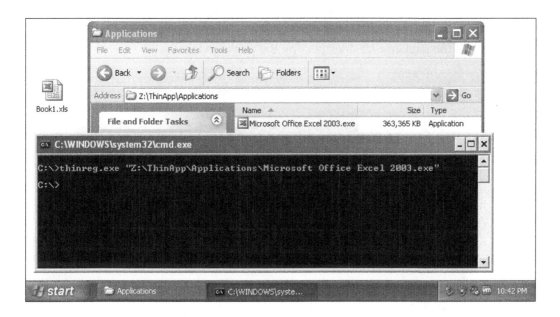

Notice that the icon changed on the `Book1.xls` file after running `thinreg.exe`, as shown in the previous screenshot.

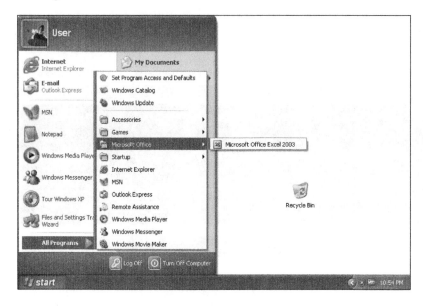

In the previous screenshot, notice that a shortcut has been created pointing to the package. In this case, the package is still located on the network share. `thinreg.exe` only registers the package - it doesn't copy the package locally.

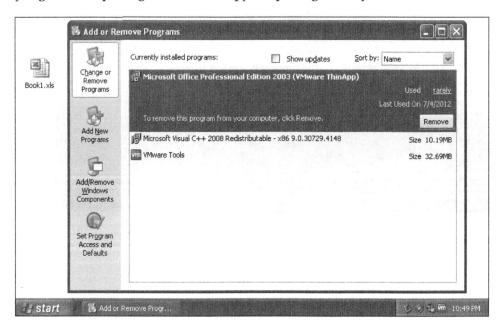

By default when running `thinreg.exe`, **Add or Remove Programs** is updated. The ThinApp packages are identified with **(VMware ThinApp)**, since you may already have the application natively installed.

`thinreg.exe` supports using wildcards. The following are a couple of examples of running `thinreg.exe`:

- `thinreg.exe \\ServerName\ShareName\*.exe`

  This command will register any package located on the share.

- `thinreg.exe \\ServerName\ShareName\*\*.exe`

  `thinreg.exe` will register all the packages located one folder down on the share.

- `thinreg.exe \\ServerName\ShareName\*\*\*.exe`

  `thinreg.exe` will register all the packages located two folders down on the share.

`thinreg.exe` supports the `PermittedGroups` parameter in `Package.ini`. If the user is not a member of the correct Active Directory group, then `thinreg.exe` will not register the package. This is especially powerful when using `thinreg.exe` with wildcards. You can have `thinreg.exe` scanning your whole ThinApp repository, only registering the packages that the user is entitled to.

`thinreg.exe` has a couple of switches for customization. If you run `thinreg.exe` without any switches, you will get the help file explaining all possible switches.

- `/a or /allusers`

  This switch will register the package machine wide, that is, for all the users. By default, `thinreg.exe` only registers the package for the current user.

- `/k or /keepunauthorized or /keep`

  This will keep registrations of the packages that the user is no longer entitled to use. Entitlement depends on the `PermittedGroups` parameter in the `Package.ini` file. By default, `thinreg.exe` will unregister the packages you are no longer entitled to.

- `/q or /quiet`

  This switch tells `thinreg.exe` not to print information to the screen.

- `/r or /reregister`

  The `reregister` switch will run registration on a package, even if the package is already registered. Note that re-registering is more time consuming than running a normal registration.

- `/u` or `/unregister` or `/uninstall`

  This is the switch to unregister a package. When unregistering a package, the unregister VBScript stored in `%AppData%\Thinstall\UnRegister` is used to revert the client's settings. If you are interested in learning what registering a package actually does to your clients, you can reverse engineer the unregister VBScripts.

- `/e` or `/exclude`

  This switch tells `thinreg.exe` what not to register. This can be both folders and packages.

- `/f` or `/file`

  You can specify a file to pass `thinreg.exe` extra parameters/switches. This is very handy if you want to update your `thinreg.exe` logic from a central location without changing your login scripts.

- `/norelaunch`

  This switch will not allow `thinreg.exe` to re-launch using elevated privileges.

- `/noarp`

  This switch will disable creation of an entry in the **Add or Remove Programs** window in **Control Panel**.

- `/nodesktoprefresh`

  Using `/nodesktoprefresh` will not refresh the users desktop. If you run multiple `thinreg.exe` parameters one after another in a login script, the desktop will refresh after each `thinreg.exe` execution. This takes time and can be irritating for the users since the screen appears to be flickering. To avoid this issue, use this switch each time you call `thinreg.exe` except the last time.

`thinreg.exe` is included in the MSI file generated by ThinApp. The obvious difference between using `thinreg.exe` standalone and MSI is that MSI copies the package to the local client's hard drive where as `thinreg.exe` doesn't. Both the techniques will register the package. The `thinreg.exe` standalone is often used when streaming your packages from a network share.

Using `thinreg.exe` with a wildcard search on a large ThinApp repository will take some time. You should make sure your login script runs in the background, not blocking the user from getting access to his or her desktop. Many examples of `thinreg.exe` login scripts can be found on the ThinApp blog, `http://blogs.vmware.com/thinapp/scripts`. One alternative is to use the ThinApp SDK (software development kit). The ThinApp SDK is freely available at the VMware web page, `http://communities.vmware.com/community/vmtn/developer/forums/thinapp`. Using the SDK will speed up registration significantly. `thinreg.exe` must open the package file in order to investigate it, while the ThinApp SDK can use APIs to investigate the package. Using the ThinApp SDK will require you to distribute and load a DLL on all clients. An example registration script using the SDK can be found at `http://blogs.vmware.com/thinapp/2012/03/configuring-the-thinapp-sdk-in-place-of-thinreg.html`.

Summary

In this chapter you've learned the different methods of deploying ThinApp packages. Hopefully you can appreciate the flexibility that ThinApp offers and choose the deployment method(s) that best suit your environment. In the next chapter, you will learn how to apply updates to existing projects.

4

Updating and Tweaking Your ThinApp Project

In previous chapters you have learned about ThinApp basics; how to create a package and how to deploy a package to your end users. Now, it's time to learn how to maintain a package. An application's life cycle includes updating the application to a new version or changing its settings. In this chapter you will learn about the following topics:

- The most efficient update method for different update needs
- How to use the sbmerge.exe tool to update a project folder
- Different sandbox considerations when creating a new version of a package

Different categories of updates

There are different categories of updates. Different update methods are preferred for different update categories. That said, a certain update mechanism may be the most efficient in a certain update scenario but can very well still be used in another. The different update categories are:

- **Major updates** (that is, full version updates): This update category is typically a major product version update. For example, Microsoft Office 2007 was updated to Microsoft Office 2010.

- **Minor updates** (typically point releases or service packs): This category typically features updates and bug fixes within a specific full version. For example, updating from Adobe Acrobat Reader 8.0 to 8.1. Both are within the full version of 8.

- **Patching** and **hotfixes**: These updates are typically smaller in size than minor updates/point releases but are essentially within the same update category.

- **Configuration changes**: Configuration changes are typically a very small number of changes. These are often only a couple of registry changes or a change to a .ini or configuration file.

- **ThinApp runtime updates**: There is rarely any need to update the ThinApp runtime within a package that is deployed and fully functional. The only reason to update the runtime would be to inject new operating system support or to update the license key in an existing package.

Recapturing an application

One update mechanism is of course to create a completely new capture of the application. I would recommend using this method only to capture a major update of an application or if you are using **Horizon Application Manager**. (More on the Horizon part in a second). When performing a full new capture, all default settings within your project folder will be different from the older version. Any customization you made to your old project has to be re-applied to the new project folder. If you want the new package to re-use the existing sandbox, that is, preserve the users' settings, you must make sure to change the SandboxName parameter in the Package.ini file, using the same name as the old package. Recapture of an application is recommended when packaging a whole new version. Upgrading from Microsoft Office 2007 to Microsoft Office 2010 is a good example of when we want to perform a full recapture. Conventionally, the major upgrade of an application such as Microsoft Office is often a case where an administrator uninstalls the old version before installing the new version due to the number of complexities within the application and the upgrade process. Taking this into account, I recommend performing a full recapture of the application. Other common Package.ini settings to consider when recapturing an application are MSIProductCode and MSIUpgradeCode. These two parameters will allow for the new version to replace old versions when deployed locally using MSI.

If you're using Horizon Application Manager to manage your ThinApp packages, you can create an update package while running **Setup Capture**.

In ThinApp Version 4.7.2, **Setup Capture** was updated with this new feature. While enabling Horizon management, you can choose to create a package that is identified as an updated version of an already existing package. When adding the new update package to Horizon, Horizon Application Manager will automatically update all entitlements with the latest version. For more details about the update mechanism in Horizon, please refer to http://kb.vmware.com/kb/2030248. You can also use relink with the -h parameter to create an update package.

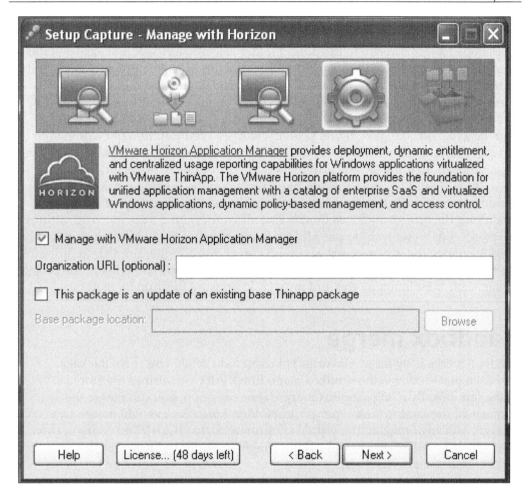

With ThinApp 4.7.2, a new feature was introduced in **Setup Capture**. You can create an updated version of a package managed by VMware Horizon Application Manager. Enable the **This package is an update of an existing base Thinapp package** option and browse browse to the folder containing the original version of your base package. This will extract the necessary App ID properties of the base package and include them as identifiers in the new package. Horizon will use these properties to identify the package as an update.

Modifying the project folder

Applying changes directly to the project folder is a very efficient and easy method of updating your packages. This method is mostly used when applying configuration changes, and patching and hotfixes. Using this update method requires that you know where changes are to be applied and how. If the configuration change is a simple change of a registry key, it's easy enough to open the registry text file, find the key, and change it. If you need to change a configuration file within your virtual environment, it's a simple matter of opening the file in Notepad and making the modification. If the update is delivered to you as files with documentation on where they should be copied, many times replacing the existing versions, case, I would personally use this method of updating. One big advantage of using the modifying the project folder method is that all your original `Package.ini` settings are preserved. If you want to use MSI for deployment of the new version, you only need to change the `MSIProductVersion` parameter to a higher number in order for the new MSI to replace existing deployments. Any previous tweaking of the project folder, such as isolation modes and more, is kept using this update method.

Sandbox merge

Sandbox merge is by far my favorite ThinApp tool. When you run a package and change its settings, the sandbox is modified. All new settings are stored in the sandbox. By using sandbox merge (`sbmerge.exe`), you can merge the contents of the sandbox into your project folder. `sbmerge.exe` will merge any changes you've applied to the virtual environment, that is, patches, configuration changes, or updates. Let me walk you through an example. Hopefully, it will demonstrate the power of `sbmerge.exe`.

Let's say we need to update the version of Mozilla Firefox we've got. In this example we'll package an update to Mozilla Firefox Version 3.6.3. This is shown in the following steps:

1. Launch the virtualized Mozilla Firefox. Luckily, Mozilla Firefox has a built-in update mechanism, so let's make use of it.

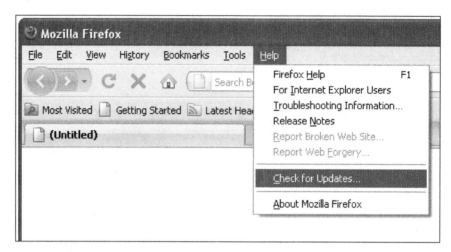

2. Run the built-in update mechanism of Mozilla Firefox.

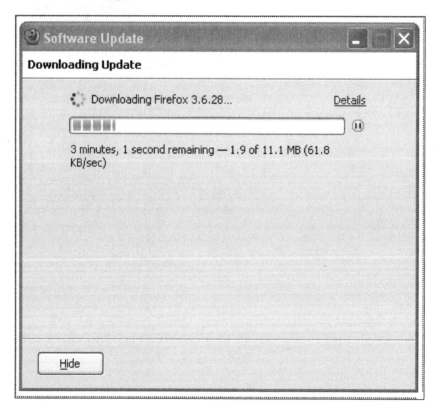

3. When you are prompted with the following screenshot, proceed by clicking on **Restart Firefox**:

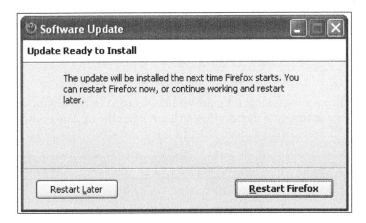

The whole update is now running within the virtual environment. All changes made by the update are stored in the sandbox.

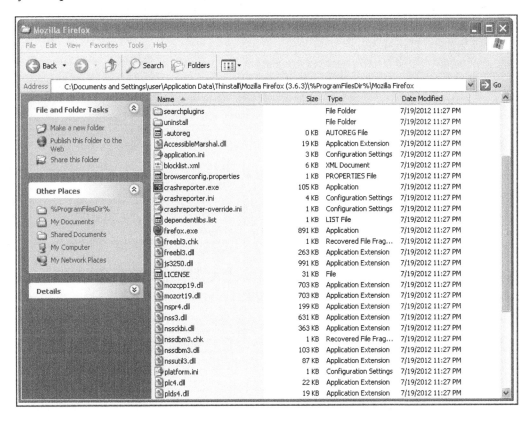

Launching the original package (Mozilla Firefox 3.6.3), using the sandbox containing the updated version of Mozilla Firefox, will run the latest version, in this case Version 3.6.28. Just to clarify what is now happening – your package's read-only data contains Mozilla Firefox 3.6.3. while your sandbox content is the Mozilla Firefox 3.6.28 update. So if you launch your Mozilla Firefox package with the updated sandbox you will be running the later version of Mozilla Firefox.

 Everything changed by the update is stored in the sandbox. You can investigate the sandbox to learn what the update changed.

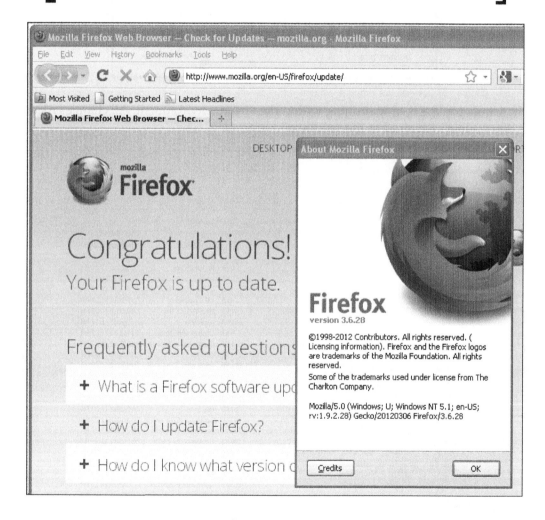

So, the combined environment of the read-only virtual environment built into the package, and the read and write part of the virtual environment stored in the sandbox, provides Version 3.6.28 of Mozilla Firefox.

Let's use `sbmerge.exe` to merge the content of the sandbox into our original project folder, creating a project folder with Mozilla Firefox 3.6.28.

`sbmerge.exe` must be launched outside the virtual environment using the command prompt. The easiest method is to navigate to the project folder and launch `sbmerge.exe` from there. If launched in the project folder, `sbmerge.exe` will automatically find its active sandbox. Launching `sbmerge.exe` using the apply switch will merge the sandbox into the project folder.

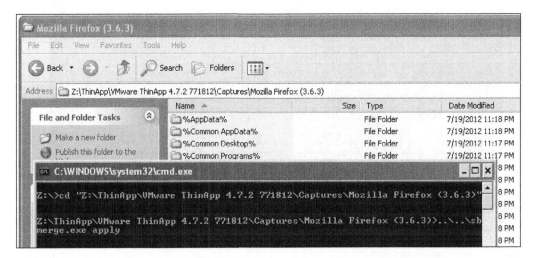

 `sbmerge.exe` is located in the ThinApp utility folder. The process involved with `sbmerge.exe` is a destructive method of updating the project folder. All conflicts will be replaced with the sandbox content, so make sure you always have a backup copy of your project folder.

During the sandbox merge, you'll be presented with all the changes being applied to your project folder, as shown in the following screenshot:

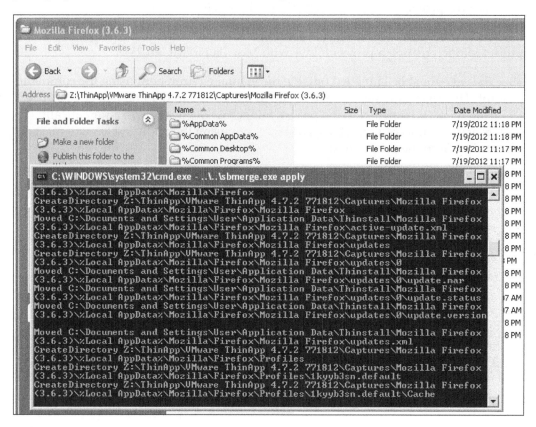

When the sbmerge.exe process is finished, you will only have to rebuild your project folder to create the new version of your package.

I hope the previous example shows you the process and the power of using `sbmerge.exe`. It's a quick and simple way of applying changes to existing packages. And it's not only for applying updates. Simple configuration changes can be applied to the project folder in seconds. Launch the packaged application, change the settings, shut down the application, and run `sbmerge.exe`. Easy peasy! `sbmerge.exe` is suitable for minor updates, patching and hotfixes, and configuration changes.

Manually editing the project folder's registry files is not the most user-friendly method for changing the virtual registry. When I have to modify the registry, I tend to use a **regedit.exe** entry point and make use of `sbmerge.exe`.

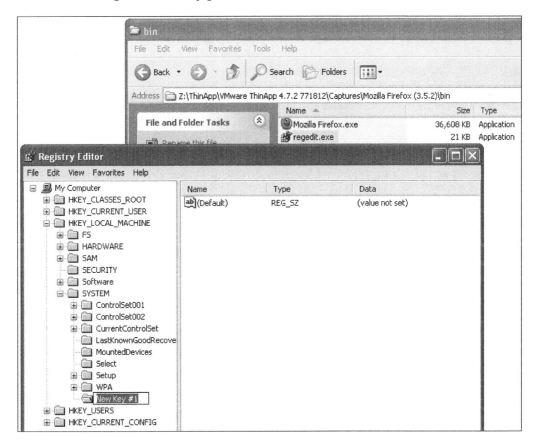

Running `regedit.exe` within the virtual environment will update the virtual registry.

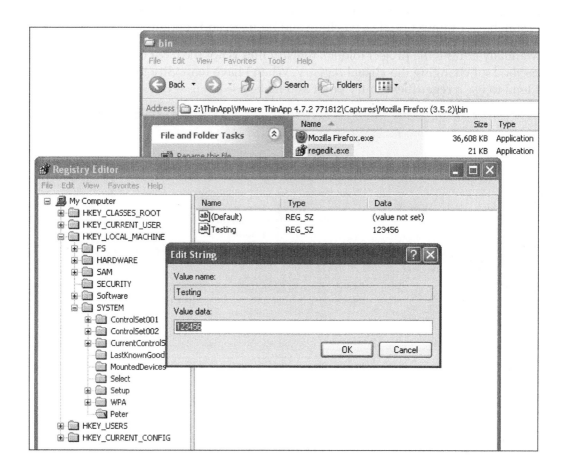

When prompted with the **Edit String** dialog box, I added the key, **Peter**, and created a value called **Testing**, as shown in the previous screenshot.

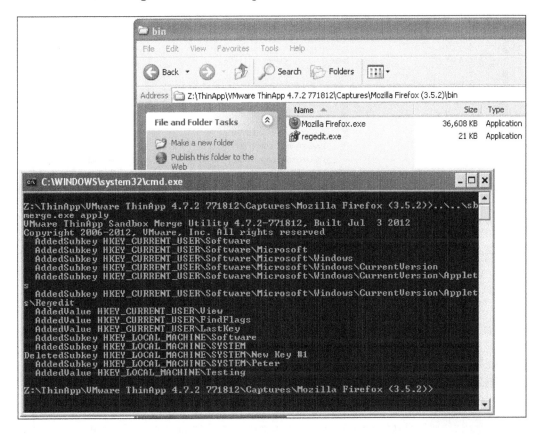

Run sbmerge.exe to merge the registry changes into the project folder.

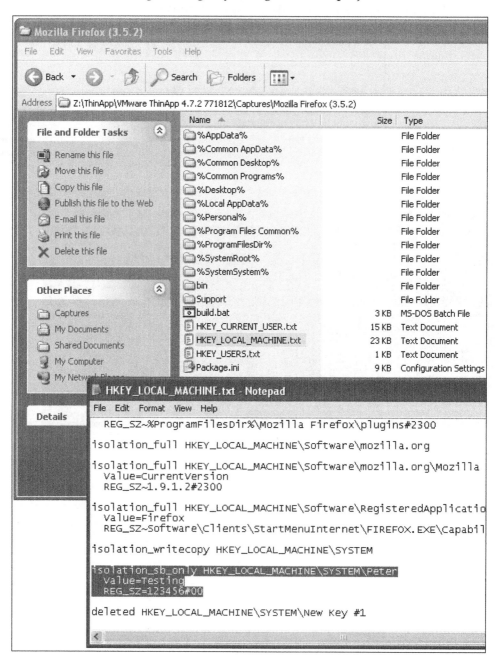

After a successful `sbmerge.exe` execution, you can find the registry entries within the registry file.

As mentioned earlier, the easiest method is to be standing in the project folder when running `sbmerge.exe`. You can be located anywhere and point to the location of the project folder, and the sandbox using `-ProjectDir` or `-SandboxDir` switches. But I find it much easier running `sbmerge.exe` standing in the project folder. Then, I don't have to worry about getting the paths correct.

You can run `sbmerge.exe` in one of two ways. The first one is `sbmerge.exe PRINT`, and that will not alter your project folder. It will only run the comparison between the sandbox and the project folder. I tend to run the command and redirect the output to a text file, for example, `sbmerge.exe PRINT > c:\output.txt`. This way, I can read what is different and what a certain update has modified. Then, once you want to merge the sandbox content into the project folder, you can run `sbmerge.exe APPLY`. When the sandbox merge has completed successfully, the sandbox is deleted.

You should use a copy of your project folder. `sbmerge.exe` is a destructive update mechanism and there is no way to revert changes applied to the project folder.

Make sure you always start with a clean sandbox when applying the changes that you want to merge into your project folder. You do not want to pollute the project folder with old cache files or other rubbish. You can run `sbmerge.exe` with an exclusion list, just like `snapshot.ini`, but I find it much easier to just make sure that the sandbox is clean. Run `sbmerge.exe` without any switches to get the help file covering all the switches you can use.

While using sandbox merge, it is important to use WriteCopy as the default directory isolation mode within the package. It is difficult to tell upfront where changes will be made, so sandboxing everything is your safest bet.

Updating the ThinApp runtime

You can update the ThinApp runtime embedded in the packages. You can rebuild your project folder using a new ThinApp version, or you can use the tool relink. exe to update the runtime. relink.exe does not require the project folder. It will apply a new runtime directly into an existing package. There's rarely any need to update the ThinApp runtime. Normally, you don't need to update your packages when a new ThinApp version is released. But when ThinApp 4.5 was released, one of the big new features was Windows 7 support. Old packages had to be updated in order to work on Windows 7. Windows 7 (and Windows 2008 R2) was a major recoding of the operating system with many Windows API changes, and therefore the ThinApp runtime had to be updated. There is no telling whether the future Windows versions will force you to update runtimes for existing packages or not. Other than for operating system support, you may also want to update the runtime because you want to change the license key. While updating the runtime you can change the **License Key** and the **Licensed display name** that is displayed as well. All project folders are completely license-anonymous. If you capture an application using a trial version of ThinApp, you can simply change the license information, and rebuild or use relink.exe to transform your packages into fully licensed versions.

You can change the **License Key** or **Licensed display name** by launching **Setup Capture**, clicking on the top-left corner, and choosing **License...**.

Enter your new information in the **Enter License Key** dialog box, as shown in the following screenshot:

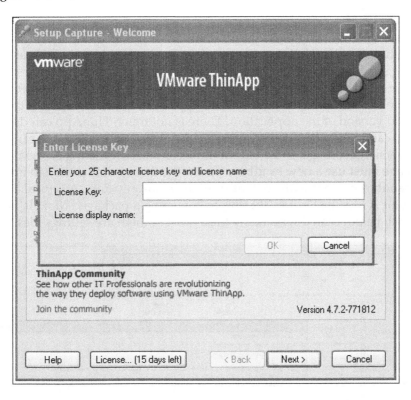

`relink.exe` is great for batch-updating your whole ThinApp repository. `relink.exe` can scan for packages to update recursively.

```
relink.exe -Recursive "Z:\ThinApp Repository"
```

This command will scan recursively and update all packages and MSI files found.

With ThinApp 4.7.2, `relink.exe` was updated with a new feature: **Horizon Application Manager** support. With `relink.exe -h`, you can add Horizon management to an existing package without needing to rebuild the whole project. In this knowledge-base article, you can find much more detail about the `-h` switch: http://kb.vmware.com/kb/2021928.

If you type `relink.exe` without any switches at a command prompt, you'll get the help text for `relink.exe`.

When you run `relink.exe`, make sure you have enough free disk space. `relink.exe` will make a backup of the original package before updating the package.

Sandbox considerations for updated packages

When updating an existing package, you must consider the existing sandbox. In many situations, you might want to preserve the users' settings and therefore reuse the existing sandbox. Make sure the new version of the package uses the same SandboxName and SandboxPath values, and the existing sandbox will be used, that is, if the new version of the virtualized application can handle the settings from the old version of the application. There is not much ThinApp can do if the application cannot handle existing settings. Luckily, most applications can handle previous versions' settings. If the old sandbox contains conflicting elements, your new package must use a new sandbox. Currently, there is no method to update the existing sandbox content with content from the read-only data. A typical example of this behavior is Mozilla Firefox. By simply launching a packaged Mozilla Firefox, the sandbox will be populated with many files. Most of them are settings files.

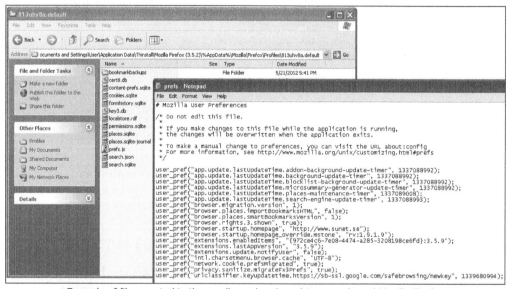

Example of files created in the sandbox when launching a packaged Mozilla Firefox

As you can see in the previous screenshot, the **prefs.js** file is created in the user's sandbox. **pref.js** holds many Mozilla Firefox settings. One of the settings is the homepage. You can't enforce a new homepage in a new Mozilla Firefox package. Since **prefs.js** is already present in the sandbox, the version stored in the package will not be used. There are a couple of different methods you can use as workarounds for this.

- Use a new sandbox and merge settings from the existing sandbox. For example, a script can be used to copy content from the old sandbox into the new one.

- Store the user settings outside the virtual environment, that is, use Merged on `%AppData%`. This way, you can use traditional, physical methods to change users' settings.

- Implement a VBScript in the new package, altering the settings you want to enforce.

The most important thing is that you are aware of a certain package's behavior. That is why it's so important to investigate the sandbox when you're test running a package. You must know what will end up in the sandbox and investigate if it will be an issue later on when updating.

Summary

In this chapter you have learned how to create a new version of a package. There are many different methods you can use, and some are more suitable for certain update categories than others. The next chapter will explain how to deploy these new versions of your packages.

5

How to Distribute Updates

In the previous chapter you learned how to create a new version of a package. This chapter will guide you through the different methods of getting the new version to your end users.

This chapter will cover the following topics:

- Using MSI to deploy updates
- In-place update
- How to use AppLink for updates
- Application Sync
- How to distribute updates with VMware Horizon Application Manager

Different categories of updates

The different update categories specified in the previous chapter are still very much valid when talking about deployment methods for updates. So first let's start with a quick recap of the different categories as I see it:

- **Major updates** (that is, full version updates): This update category is typically a major product version update. For example, Microsoft Office 2007 updated to Office 2010.

- **Minor updates** (typically point releases or service packs): This category is typically feature updates and bug fixes within a specific full version. For example, updating from Adobe Acrobat Reader 8.0 to 8.1. Both are within the full version of 8.

- **Patching and hotfixes**: These updates are typically smaller in size than minor updates/point releases but are essentially within the same update category.

- **Configuration changes**: Configuration changes typically involve very few changes. These are often only a couple of registry changes or a change to an .ini configuration file.

- **ThinApp Runtime updates**: There is rarely any need to update the ThinApp Runtime within a package that is deployed and fully functional. The only reason to update the runtime would be to inject new operating system support or updating the license key in an existing package. Normally when a new ThinApp release is made available you do not bother updating existing, deployed packages.

It is important to understand that when you create a new version of a package and use one of the update methods described in this chapter, all package settings are from the new package. Things such as Sandbox location and name or installation location are all from the new version's `Package.ini`.

Using MSI to distribute updates

Using MSI as the deployment method for your updates fits all categories of updates, since it reuses existing processes. If you deploy new applications and packages with the help of MSI, why not use the same process for deploying updates? I fully understand that kind of reasoning. Using MSI might not be the most effective method when taking bandwidth and speed into consideration, but using processes already in place are often more important. Using MSI to deploy a new version of your package will require the whole package to be downloaded by your clients. The MSI that ThinApp generates is capable of replacing existing deployments. The parameters in use for a successful replacement of existing packages are `MSIProductVersion`, `MSIProductCode`, and `MSIUpgradeCode` found in the MSI section of `Package.ini`. If you create your new version of the package by modifying the old project folder, you should only have to activate and change the `MSIProductVersion` value, providing it with a higher number. If the `MSIProductCode` and `MSIUpgradeCode` parameters are left disabled, the ThinApp build process will make sure to handle the correct **Globally Unique Identifier** (**GUID**). GUIDs are application-unique identifiers. If your new version is using a new project folder you must manually make sure that the new package uses the same `MSIUpgradeCode` parameter as the old package. The `MSIProductCode` should be different in the two packages.

Let's have a look at a couple of versions of the `Package.ini` file explaining the process of creating an update MSI file.

The following is `Package.ini` for Version 1.0 (original version):

```
[BuildOptions]
;-------- MSI Parameters ----------
;EnableMSIFilename if you want to generate a Windows Installer
package.
```

```
;MSIFilename=Mozilla Firefox (3.5.2).msi
;MSIManufacturer=Corp Inc.
MSIProductVersion=1.0
;MSIDefaultInstallAllUsers=1
;MSIRequireElevatedPrivileges=1
;MSIInstallDirectory=Mozilla Firefox (3.5.2) (VMware ThinApp)
;MSIProductCode={A52D0259-C701-A136-6C62-8C5935820679}
;MSIUpgradeCode={824D99C2-9F8E-B59D-DB98-18817BE5FD42}
;MSIStreaming=0
;MSICompressionType=Fast
;MSIArpProductIcon=%ProgramFilesDir%\Mozilla Firefox\firefox.exe,0
```

The following is `Package.ini` for Version 1.1 (updated version):

```
[BuildOptions]
;-------- MSI Parameters ----------
;EnableMSIFilename if you want to generate a Windows Installer
package.
;MSIFilename=Mozilla Firefox (3.5.2).msi
;MSIManufacturer=Corp Inc.
MSIProductVersion=1.1
;MSIDefaultInstallAllUsers=1
;MSIRequireElevatedPrivileges=1
;MSIInstallDirectory=Mozilla Firefox (3.5.2) (VMware ThinApp)
;MSIProductCode={A52D0259-C701-A136-6C62-8C5935820679}
;MSIUpgradeCode={824D99C2-9F8E-B59D-DB98-18817BE5FD42}
;MSIStreaming=0
;MSICompressionType=Fast
;MSIArpProductIcon=%ProgramFilesDir%\Mozilla Firefox\firefox.exe,0
```

The previous example will successfully uninstall the existing Version 1.0 of packaged Mozilla Firefox and deploy Version 1.1 of the package.

 I'm disabling the `MSIProductCode` and `MSIUpgradeCode` parameters, leaving the ThinApp build process to handle them.

Once you've created your updated MSI file you can use any existing deployment tool to distribute the update. One of the benefits of using ThinApp is that there's not much that can go wrong when you deploy an update. It's just a matter of replacing the package, many times by just copying one single file. You don't have to change registry keys, risk introducing regression, or worry about the update mysteriously stopping after 90 percent is done.

Using an in-place update method

In-place update is truly my favorite among update deployment methods. It's a feature that is unique to ThinApp and truly makes the most use of application virtualization. The feature in-place update has been called many things over the years. You will find references using the name integer update or side-by-side update. I personally prefer the name in-place update so that's the name I will use. In-place update is most effective when using the streaming deployment method. When you use streaming as your deployment method, your environment will have only one single instance of the application, represented by the package located on a network share. So for you to update the version deployed you simply have to replace this one single instance with the new updated version. But what happens if the package is in use? When a ThinApp package is launched the file is locked. You cannot delete it or replace it. That's when in-place update comes in handy. In-place update will allow you to deploy the new version next to the old version with zero downtime, during full production. Upon the next launch of the package the ThinApp runtime will find the in-place update package and, seamless to the user, will shutdown the old version of the Package and launch the new updated package instead. Let's have a look at how this works:

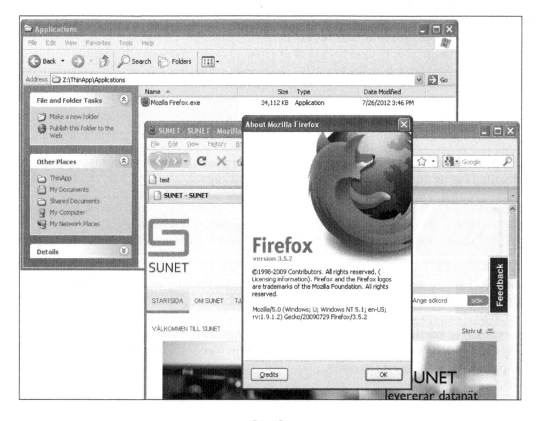

The previous image shows Version 3.5.2 of **Mozilla Firefox** deployed to my ThinApp repository.

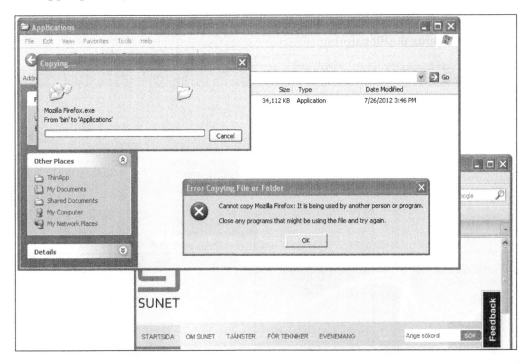

If I keep the Mozilla Firefox package running in the background and try to replace the version of the Mozilla Firefox package, I am not allowed to do so since the package is in use.

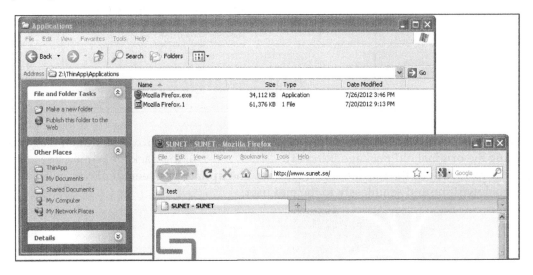

So instead we use in-place update and rename the updated package, in this case containing Version 3.6.28 of **Mozilla Firefox**, to use a number as an extension instead of `.exe`. Now the filename is not conflicting, and both packages can be located in the same folder. Please note the size difference between the two versions. My old version of **Mozilla Firefox** is still running.

When the end users shut down the old version of Mozilla Firefox and launch it again, using the original old package (`Mozilla Firefox.exe`), the package named `Mozilla Firefox.1` will be the one launched instead. The update has been deployed with zero downtime and seamlessly to the end user.

In-place update works just as great for downgrades. Let's say you found an issue in the newly deployed Version 3.6.28 of Mozilla Firefox and needed to immediately revert to the old version.

Create a copy of the old version of the Mozilla Firefox package, give it a higher number than the previous package as its file extension. Now the original version becomes the new active package. Please note the file size to identify the copy of Version 3.5.2 now named `Mozilla Firefox.2`. You must keep the original `Mozilla Firefox.exe` package since that's the one the end user's shortcut and registration information points to.

Deploying many updates, and perhaps reverting some, will leave quite a few copies of packages in your ThinApp repository. As soon as the not active in-place versions are not in use anymore, you can safely delete those. During your planned service window you can clean up your ThinApp repository, replacing the original `PackageName.exe` file with the latest active version. When performing in-place updates, it is important to understand that it's the data container that needs to be updated. If you have a package using a separate data container, you must update the data container using an in-place update. The entry points do not have to be updated for the new version of the virtual environment to be activated.

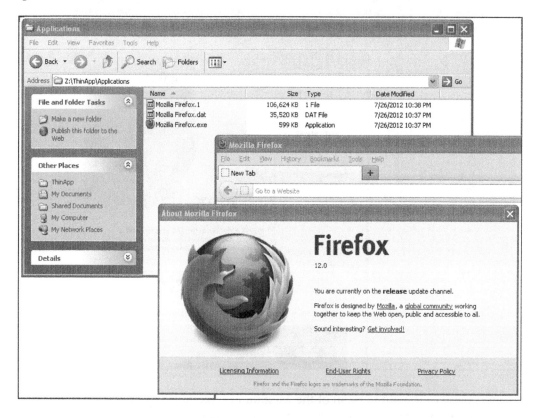

In the previous image, I'm in-place updating a package using a separate data container. This is an in-place update of Mozilla Firefox Version 3.5.9 (`Mozilla Firefox.dat`) with Version 12.0 of Mozilla Firefox (`Mozilla Firefox.1`).

When using in-place update to update packages with a separate data container it's best practice to make sure that the entry point and the data container don't have the same name. In my previous example I've used the same name for both the data container and the entry point (both names are Mozilla Firefox before the extension). It still works, but you get an irritating command prompt launching the in-place updated package.

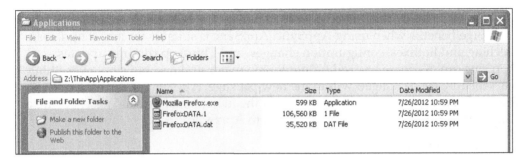

Best practice when in-place updating a package using a separate data container is to have different names for the entry point and data container.

In-place update is the most suitable method for delivering Major, Minor, and ThinApp Runtime updates when using Streaming deployment method. It will of course work for deployment of the other update types as well, but might not be the most efficient method available.

You do not have to store the in-place update packages next to the original package if you don't want to. You can change the location of your in-place updates by specifying the UpgradePath parameter in Package.ini.

The in-place update method works on your AppLink packages as well. I hope this description of the in-place update makes you as excited about the feature as I am. I just love demoing it for customers. It's always a hit.

Application Sync (AppSync)

Application Sync or AppSync is another unique ThinApp update method. AppSync was designed to help deal with the management of applications on unmanaged devices. Typical case of usage is a consultant having his/her own computer, and you have to provide an application to the consultant. Using AppSync you are able to maintain the application on the consultant's machine without the need of a locally installed management agent. AppSync can be run with the help of the standalone tool, AppSync.exe found in the ThinApp utilities folder. But most of the time you use the built-in AppSync feature in your packages.

When a package has AppSync activated, it will check for an updated version of itself when it's started. The check for update and the download of any updated version all happens in the background, seamless to the user. If there's a new version available, the package will download only the blocks that are different. When all the changed blocks have successfully been downloaded, a new version of the package is compiled. Upon the next launch of the package, the new version replaces the old version. Being agentless (that is, it does not require anything locally installed on the clients) and its method of incrementally downloading only the changed blocks are both huge benefits when using AppSync. AppSync is suitable for minor updates, patching and hotfixes, configuration changes, and ThinApp runtime updates. AppSync can of course be used for deploying major updates, but since everything has probably been changed within the new package, AppSync will have to download the whole package and cannot make use of the incremental download. There are a couple of `Package.ini` parameters related to AppSync.

```
[BuildOptions]
;-------- AppSync Parameters ----------
;AppSyncURL=https://example.com/some/path/PackageName.exe
```

The `AppSyncURL` parameter specifies the location of the update package. You must specify the whole path to the update package's data container. HTTP, HTTPS, and FILE are supported protocols. If you use HTTPS, make sure the clients trust the certificate. There is no GUI available to the user to accept untrusted certificates. There isn't any GUI for providing authentication information either, so you can't protect your `AppSyncURL` by demanding username and password. The path to the update package has to be specified in URL format:

```
file://ServerName/ShareName/Folder/UpdatePackageDataCon.dat
```

This `AppSyncURL` example will search for new versions on a network share.

```
file:///c:/Folder/UpdatePackageDataCon.dat
```

In the above example, a local path is used as the `AppSyncURL` parameter. Please note the three forward slashes. This is the URL format for specifying a local drive. Using a local path might not be one of the most common use cases. One use case could be updating using a USB stick or CD-ROM.

The following are the remaining `Package.ini` parameters used to control AppSync functionality:

- `;AppSyncUpdateFrequency=1d`: This parameter specifies how often the package will search for updates. Valid update frequencies are: minutes (m), hours (h), or days (d). Please note that the package only checks for updates when it's launched. If the package is not used by the end user, AppSync will not update the package.

- `;AppSyncExpirePeriod=30d`: If the package has not been able to contact `AppSyncURL` within the specified time frame, it will expire. `30` days is the default setting. If you want your package to never expire, you should specify, `AppSyncExpirePeriod=never`.

- `;AppSyncWarningPeriod=5d`: The `AppSyncWarningPeriod` parameter specifies how many days ahead of expiration the package should display a warning message to the end user. The message that will be displayed is specified using the `AppSyncWarningMessage` parameter.

- `;AppSyncWarningFrequency=1d`: This parameter specifies how often the `AppSyncWarningMessage` message will be displayed. The message is only displayed at application launch.

- `;AppSyncWarningMessage=This application will become unavailable for use in %remaining_days% day(s) if it cannot contact its update server. Check your network connection to ensure uninterrupted service.`

  This message is displayed to the user to warn that the package is about to expire.

- `;AppSyncExpireMessage=This application has been unable to contact its update server for %expire_days% day(s), so it is unavailable for use. Check your network connection and try again.`

  If the package has expired then this message will be shown to the end user.

- `;AppSyncUpdatedMessage=`

  When an update has been deployed, the end user can be notified with this message.

- ;AppSyncClearSandboxOnUpdate=0

  Upon updating the package you, as an administrator, can decide to delete the existing sandbox. The default choice is to leave the existing sandbox untouched.

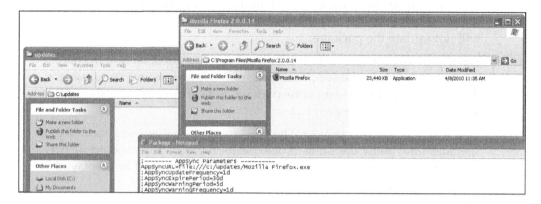

Here's an example of an AppSync-activated package. As you can see in the `Package.ini` file, I am using a local path as the `AppSyncURL`.

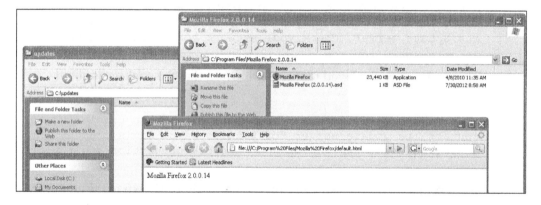

When launching a package with AppSync activated, a log file will be created (the .asd file). This log file tells the package if it managed to contact `AppSyncURL` or not. In this example there was no update package, so no AppSync action was required.

I deleted the AppSync log file to force a new AppSync operation to start at the next launch. I copied a new version of my package into the `AppSyncURL` location.

When I launch the old package it recognizes that there is a new version available. The package downloads all the changed blocks into the .ase file. The .asl file is only present while updates are being downloaded. If you close your package before everything has been downloaded the package will start where it was left last upon the next launch, thanks to the .asl file.

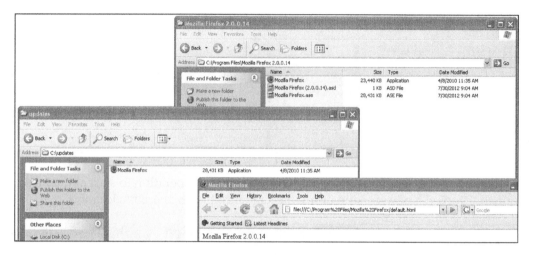

When all the changed blocks have been fetched, the ThinApp runtime will add all the unchanged blocks from the original package and create a fully functional package as the .ase file. Please note that the size of the .ase file is identical to the updated package located in the **C:\updates** folder.

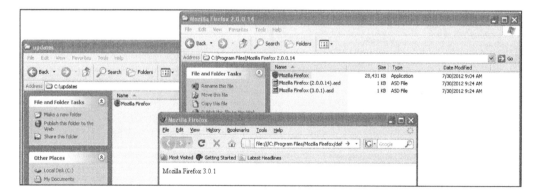

Upon the next launch, the old package is deleted and the new package is renamed to the name of the package. In this example the `InventoryName` parameter is different in the two packages, therefore a new version of the `.asd` file is created.

AppSync lacks typical enterprise features such as reporting, the ability to deploy an update ahead of time, and activating the new version on a certain date. But because of its ease of use and robustness, AppSync is getting more popular. More and more customers use AppSync as their method of deploying updates, not only to external contractors but to their managed devices as well. It doesn't matter if you skip an update, AppSync will make sure all clients run the same version eventually. Looking for updated packages is very quick. AppSync compares the hash of the packages to find out if there is an update available or not. When AppSync decides that there is an update available it will start to compare the hash of each block and only download those that are different. This method of investigating the package without downloading it is made possible by some clever coding from ThinApp developers. The fact that the Web or file server hosting the update doesn't need any locally installed components is even more impressive. The only thing you need to do if you chose to host your AppSync packages on a web server, is to make sure that the web server allows `.exe` and `.dat` files to be downloaded. On newer Microsoft IIS servers you'll have to manually configure this.

The built-in AppSync has some caveats but there are some other ways to execute an AppSync update. In order for built-in AppSync to work, both packages must have `AppSyncURL` activated. AppSync can be initiated using the ThinApp SDK. On the ThinApp SDK community page (`http://communities.vmware.com/community/vmtn/developer/forums/thinapp`) you can find example scripts and download the ThinApp SDK. Using AppSync via the ThinApp SDK or `AppSync.exe` does not require your packages to have `AppSyncURL` activated. Both methods allow you to specify an `AppSyncURL` location when you run the command allowing a dynamic `AppSyncURL`. Another benefit of not running the built-in version of AppSync is that you can run AppSync in another user context. When running the built-in AppSync, the whole AppSync operation is carried out in the context of the current user.

Using the SDK or `AppSync.exe` you can launch these AppSync operations using any user account. You can also specify when AppSync will occur, for example with the help of an AT scheduled job on your Windows clients.

In the previous picture I'm running `AppSync.exe` specifying both the `AppSyncURL` and the package to update.

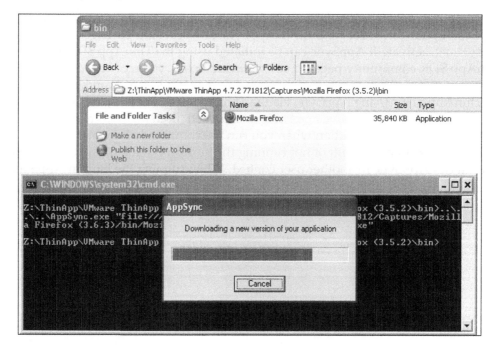

During the download of the new version you will be presented with a progress bar. Please note that the package never gets launched.

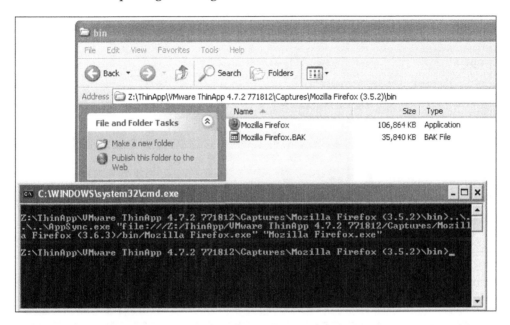

Once the update has finished the new version will be the new active package and the old version is stored as a backup using the .bak extension.

When using AppSync on a package that uses a separate data container it's important to remember to reference the data container as your AppSyncURL. The data container must not share the same filename as any entry point or AppSync will fail.

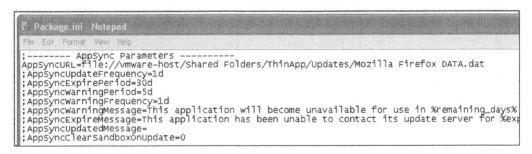

In this example I'm using a UNC path as my `AppSyncURL`, and since the package is using a separate data container, it's the data container I refer to.

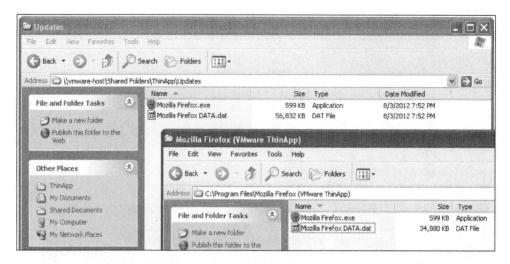

Both my original version and the updated package use a separate data container. Please note that I've named the entry point and the data container differently.

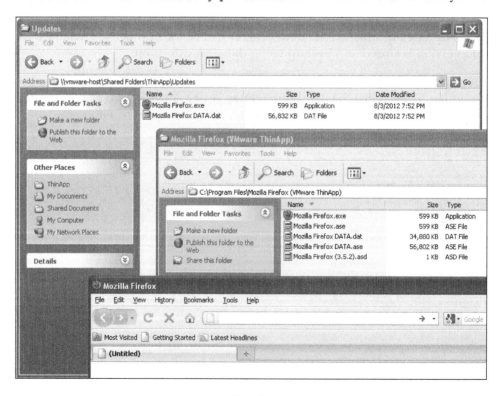

Both the new entry point and the new data container are downloaded.

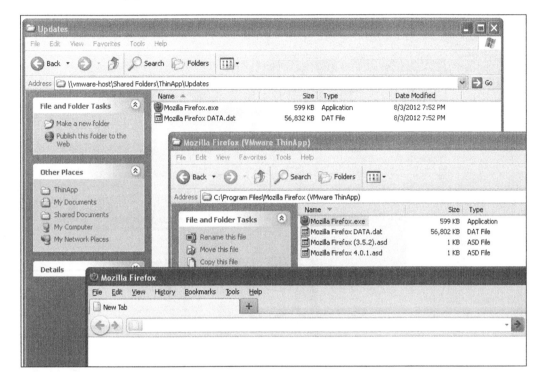

Upon the next launch of the package, the user will use the updated version.

The fact that the built-in AppSync runs in the context of the user will require the user to have the permission to modify the original version of the package. Luckily there's a workaround for this. Using `UpgradePath`, you can specify an alternative location for the AppSync log and all of the cache files. This will also hide the `.asd` file so that the end users can't as easily find the file and reactivate an expired package by deleting the log file. The end user must have permission to modify the `UpgradePath` location.

In the next example I've specified the `UpgradePath` value in my `Package.ini` file:

```
[BuildOptions]
UpgradePath=C:\ThinAppCache
```

My `AppSyncURL` looks like this:

```
AppSyncURL=file://vmware-host/Shared Folders/ThinApp/Updates/Mozilla
Firefox.exe
```

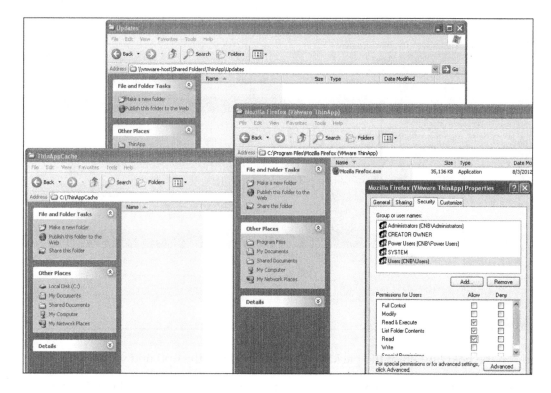

My ThinApp package, in which my user only has **Read & Execute**, **List** and **Read** privileges, is located in **C:\Program Files\Mozilla Firefox (VMware ThinApp)**.

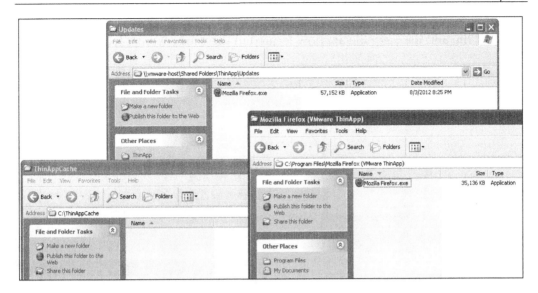

I place my updated package in the AppSyncURL location.

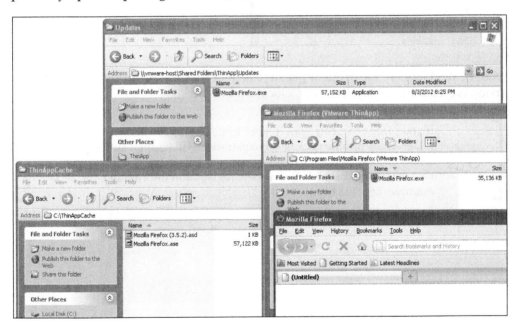

Launching my original package will start the AppSync process. As you can see, both the `.asd` file and the `.ase` file are now located in the `UpgradePath` location.

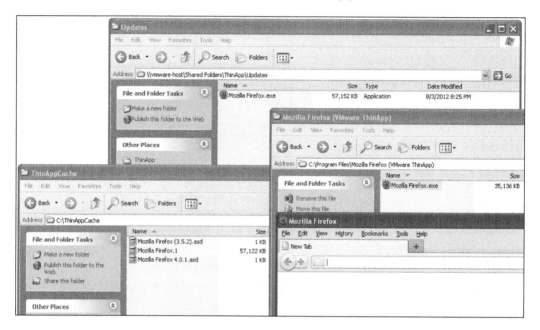

Upon the next launch, the original package is not replaced. An in-place update version is created in the `UpgradePath` location instead.

If you place `thinreg.exe` in your `AppSyncURL` location, in the same folder as the update package, a registration will happen automatically after a successful update of your package. This helps you when your new version of the package has new registration information, for example, new file types.

Application Linking (AppLink)

Yes, application linking can be considered or used as an update method. AppLink was not originally designed with this in mind, but since ThinApp runtime handles conflicting AppLink elements the way it does, it can be used to deploy updates to packages. AppLink as an update method is more or less only suitable for configuration changes. Since the update will be in a separate, somewhat loosely connected file, it's not recommended for use in applying security patches. If you don't have access to the AppLink, you will risk running an unpatched version. You can work around this by using `RequiredAppLinks`, but then you run the risk of over engineering the whole implementation. Let's repeat the AppLink conflict handling.

The last loaded conflicting element (file or registry key) will win. AppLink packages (child packages) are loaded after the parent package. Isolation modes use a different conflict handling; the most restrictive will win. So when using AppLink for updating you should make sure you're in full control of the isolation modes used. You don't want to change the isolation modes of your parent package by mistake.

The following screenshot shows a fictive example of using AppLink to update a package:

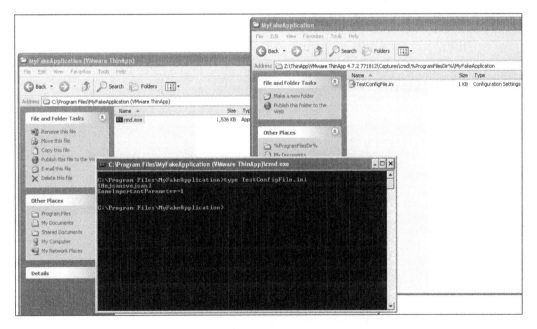

The fictive application package is deployed locally to my client. The package only contains a configuration file called TestConfigFile.ini and an entry point to CMD. EXE. I have launched the CMD entry point and used the command **type** to display the content of the file stored in the package. The Package.ini file of the package contains the OptionalAppLinks=updates*.exe parameter.

I made a copy of my original project folder and modified the TestConfigFile.ini. This will be the content of my AppLink update package. I'm still using CMD as the entry point. The source of the entry point is of no importance in this case. We must have one file storing the data container so the CMD entry point is as good as any.

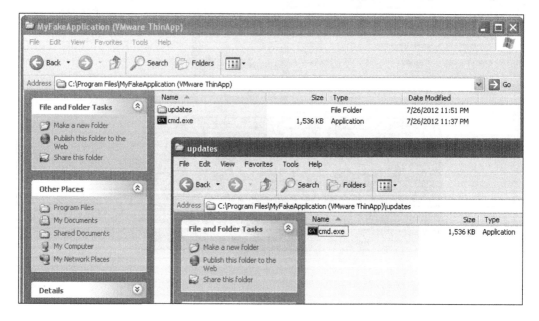

I create the AppLink location specified in the parent package's `Package.ini` file (updates folder next to the package) and copy my updated package into it.

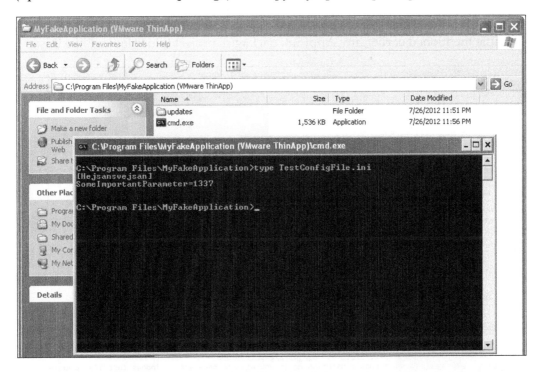

Now running the command **type** to display the content of the `TestConfigFile.ini` file will show the content of my child package's `TestConfigFile.ini`. This proves that we can use AppLink to change elements within an existing package.

Using AppLink to handle updates to the deployed packages can be a very efficient method. Let's say your deployed package is 1 GB in size. You need to change one single registry key. Creating an AppLink package containing only that one registry key will be approximately 600 KB in size. Pushing out 600 KB is much less data to deploy to your clients than if you were to copy a whole new version of the 1 GB large package.

It will require some planning ahead using AppLink for updating. You must have activated AppLink when building your package to begin with. Creating the update package requires some planning as well. The update package should not contain anything but the element/elements that it's supposed to update. In the fictive example mentioned earlier, my AppLink package's project folder looked like this:

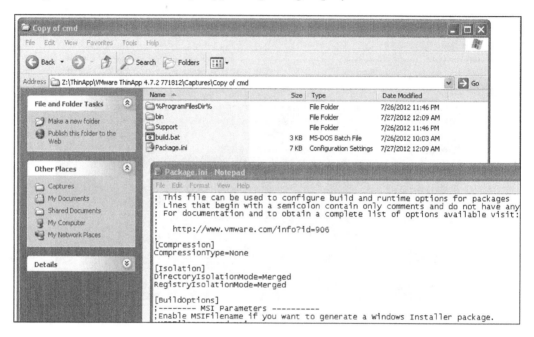

It's important to keep the AppLink update package as clean as possible to make sure you don't modify anything unintentionally. In this example, I have cleaned out everything unnecessary. All isolation modes have been set to Merged, even the registry isolation mode, guaranteeing that my update package will lose any isolation mode conflict negotiations.

Deploying updated packages using VMware Horizon Application Manager

Horizon Application Manager identifies managed ThinApp packages using Horizon-specific GUIDs built in to the package (these GUIDs are separate from the MSI-file GUIDs mentioned earlier). You generate these GUIDs when you activate Horizon Manager for a package. In order for Horizon Application Manager to identify a package as an update to an existing package, the `AppID` of the two packages must be the same. Horizon will also use another `Package.ini` parameter called `VersionID` to understand which of the packages are the latest. You can manually find the `AppID` of a package using the ThinApp SDK but it's not a very user-friendly method. Your best option is therefore to run Setup Capture specifying that you are creating an update package during the Horizon activation part of the wizard. This method will extract all the necessary information and inject them into the new package's `Package.ini` file.

Let's have a look at a Horizon implementation and how to update a package managed by Horizon Application Manager:

Here's the currently active and deployed package. You can see a GUID listed but this ID is not the one used to identify packages during update. The name of the package is `Mozilla Firefox.exe`, but since the `InventoryName` of the package is **Mozilla Firefox (3.5.2)** this will be the name displayed in Horizon's administration interface. The version of the package is known to Horizon as Version **1.0**. The Horizon environment uses **\\fileserver.pinata.local\ThinApp** as the ThinApp repository.

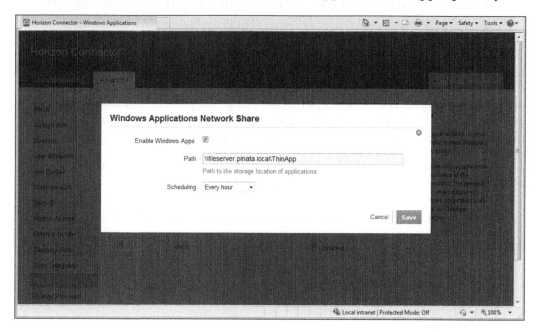

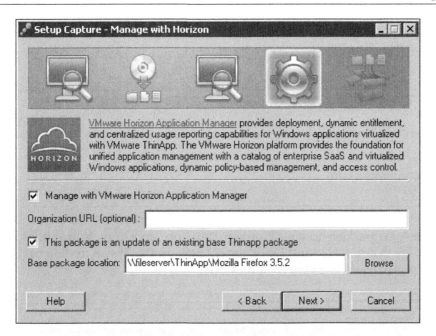

While capturing a new version of Mozilla Firefox I refer to the folder where the old version of the package exists. This will extract the necessary GUID and generate a new `VersionID` value. The new Mozilla Firefox package now includes the necessary Horizon update information.

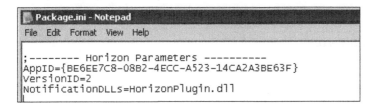

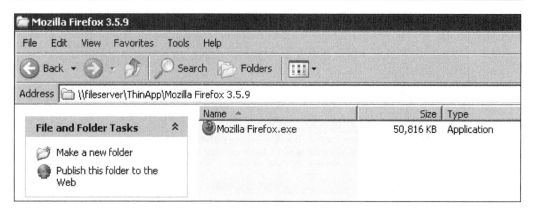

Deploy the new package to your Horizon ThinApp repository. You should place the new package in any folder and Horizon will pick up that it's an update package since the correct `AppID` and `VersionID` values exist.

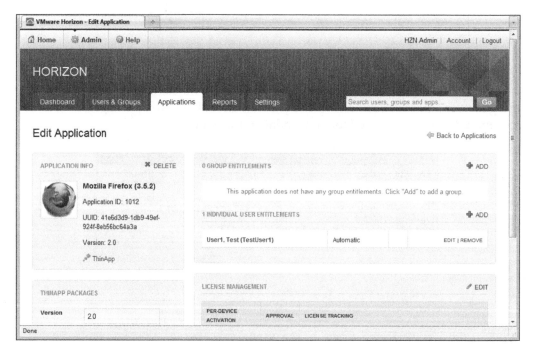

When the update package's meta data has been synchronized to Horizon, all deployments will automatically be updated. As you can see, the version is now 2.0 within the Horizon Manager. The original version's `InventoryName` is still displayed so you might want to configure the initial package accordingly.

If your deployment tool is Horizon Application Manager I would say using Horizon to deploy updates suits all the different update categories. Similar to using MSI I see a point in using the same process for deploying updates as used to deploy the packages in the first place.

Summary

This concludes the chapter on how to distribute updates. You've learned how to use different methods to deploy your new versions of ThinApp packages. There are many different methods, each with its own strength. Pick one or two that suits your environment and processes. You will probably not use all of them. Remember to keep your implementation and design simple. Just because a feature exists, it doesn't mean you must use it.

The next chapter will cover ThinApp's best practices.

6
Design and Implementation Considerations using ThinApp

In previous chapters, you've learned how to create and deploy ThinApp packages, as well as how to create and deploy updates. Now it's time to have a look at some different design and implementation consideration. This chapter is to be considered as a discussion more than best practices written in stone. ThinApp offers truly unique flexibility. The problem is that all this flexibility can become a bit overwhelming. It's hard to give you a recommended ThinApp design in this book, because all environments are unique.

In this chapter we'll discuss:

- Protecting your packages
- Isolation mode considerations
- Sandbox design
- ThinDirect
- Designing for a physical desktop, virtual desktop, or mixed environment
- Streaming share sizing

Protecting your packages

Since a ThinApp package is very portable between operating systems and clients, it's important to protect your packages from being copied and used on unauthorized devices. There are several different methods you can use to protect your packages:

- Using Active Directory groups
- Built-in VBScript
- Using VMware Horizon Application Manager
- Using third-party solutions

Protecting Packages with the help of Active Directory (AD) group membership is probably the most common method. During build time, you specify AD groups within your `Package.ini` file. You or your client must be a member of the correct group or execution will be denied. This method is very robust and secure. The downside is that it can be a bit static by nature. If you want to change the group used for protection, you must rebuild your package.

With a VBScript, virtually any logic can be used to validate if the package is allowed to execute or not. With `ExitProcess` you can terminate the package if your logic is not fulfilled. I've seen customers using scripts querying DNS servers, verifying the IP range, and with that allowing for per location-based entitlement. Remember, ThinApp is not a security product so there will always be possible workarounds to VBScript protection, but for most scenarios it's good enough.

VMware Horizon Application Manager will allow for dynamic policy management of your ThinApp packages. If you want to change entitlement, you can do so within the Horizon Administration web portal and the local Horizon Agent will poll for policy changes and apply them on the fly. Without the local Horizon Agent there is no way of executing a Horizon Enabled ThinApp package.

There are some third-party solutions available for protecting ThinApp packages. One of the most well known is the solution from Concept Software (`http://www.softwarekey.com`). The benefit of the solution from Concept Software is that it doesn't require any locally installed components. It's agentless, just like ThinApp. It requires you to wrap the original executables in their bootstrapper before compiling the project folder into a package.

Most of the previous methods for protection of your packages allow for user entitlement as well. For example, if you rely on Active Directory group for protection, `thinreg.exe` will use this information and by default, only register the packages that the user is entitled to.

Protecting your environment from being attacked by viruses is, of course, of importance. A ThinApp package could, in theory, contain a virus. If your capturing environment is infected, you could end up virtualizing parts that are infected. While there is no way telling how a virus will behave, there's a high probability that any infections will be contained within the sandbox. But the execution of the virus will be allowed. This applies to applications virtualized with ThinApp getting infected from outside the virtual environment as well. The virus will probably execute, but registry keys and affected files will be stored in the sandbox, all depending on your isolation modes of course. You should therefore have antivirus software installed on all your clients. The antivirus software can detect virus infections within your sandbox because files are stored as normal files in there. Currently, there is no antivirus software that can scan inside a package's virtual environment or that can understand the package file format. Therefore, there's little to no point in allowing your antivirus software to scan your package files. Most antivirus software will keep the operating system from accessing the package while scanning it. This slows down the launch time of a package dramatically. If policies keep you from excluding your packages from being scanned on access, a possible workaround can be to make sure your data container is stored as a separate file and not within one of your entry points.

Default isolation modes

Isolation modes are probably the most important feature of ThinApp and therefore one of the most interesting in my opinion. When it comes to configuring your packages, isolation modes are of course a centerpiece.

When I create a ThinApp package, I always start using WriteCopy as my default directory isolation mode. This way all changes I do during my test runs will end up in the sandbox. This is important because it lets you get to know the behavior of the application, that is, learn what will end up in the sandbox. Why this is important we will discuss in more detail in the next chapter. When I'm ready to compile my production ready package, I usually change the default directory isolation mode to Merged. This way, the package will act like a natively installed application. It will for many locations honor the permissions specified on the client OS. For example, if a user tries to save a document in the root of the C:, a denial dialog box will be displayed to the user instead of the file getting sandboxed.

The fact that I can switch between default directory isolation modes such as this, indicates that the default directory isolation mode has no technical importance at all for my packages. I believe this is a good best practice. If the application must have a specific isolation mode on a certain location, make sure your project folder contains this setting. Countless times I've been told that a package uses either WriteCopy or Merged as the isolation mode. There is no such statement. Most packages I've seen use all three variations of the isolation modes. What they refer to is the default directory isolation mode, but that is mostly of no technical importance.

As discussed earlier in this book, **Setup Capture** will create default isolation modes for certain locations. It's possible for **Setup Capture** to add a folder macro to the project folder, even though it hasn't been modified during the capturing process. This behavior will allow most applications to run ThinApp out of the box. Another benefit is the fact you can run these *out of the box* captured applications without risking your physical environment. Most default locations use WriteCopy. A ThinApp packager is expected to investigate all isolation modes and all folder macros. It's expected that you delete the folder macros not used by your application (but leave %SystemSystem%\ Spool or your package will not be able to print) and adjust the isolation modes as needed. If your packaged application requires a specific isolation mode on a location, make sure you document this. If you add AppLink packages later, you will want to make sure that these don't change the isolation modes unintentionally.

Sandbox considerations

To be sandboxed or not to be sandboxed? That is the question. In my opinion, the smaller the sandbox is, the better. Just because ThinApp offers the sandbox functionality, I can see no reason to sandbox everything. I use the sandbox when there is a true design or application functionality reason to use it. However, client design reasons could dictate you to store as much as possible in the sandbox. You may not have a profile management tool in place or you have the need to keep the client environment absolutely clean. For you to able to revert your package into a vanilla state by simply deleting the sandbox might also be a reason.

All are very valid reasons for keeping as much as possible in the sandbox. You may not have profile management in place or the need to keep the client environment absolutely clean. Both are very valid reasons for keeping as much as possible in the sandbox. But if you already have a profile management tool in place, or simply have dedicated hardware per user and don't care if the profiles are lost, I would challenge you to think twice before you decide to sandbox everything. Whatever your environment looks like, you should have a good reason for sandboxing. You should not sandbox everything simply because that's the default behavior of a ThinApp package. Remember what was discussed earlier in this book. Any conflicting elements already in the user's sandbox will override the content of your package. This will make it harder for you to design your updated package.

I'm often asked if one should include a version number in the sandbox name or not. My answer is that it depends on the situation. If you want to preserve user settings between updates, I would get rid of the version in the sandbox name. This way, you don't risk running Version 10 of Mozilla Firefox while the active sandbox is named Mozilla Firefox 3.5.9. On the other hand, if you want to make sure you are in total control of the environment when deploying a new version, you should keep the version in the sandbox name, forcing users to create a new sandbox when launching the latest version.

All packages will have to be updated at some point in time. If modifications are made to virtualized elements, there's not much to do but sandbox the modification. A possible workaround could be to leave the element outside the virtualized package. Which is okay. A complete desktop client design will incorporate both the virtual environment within your packages and the physical environment. Too often, a client design handles them as two completely isolated topics. The two can, and often should, work together. When you package an application for native installation you're taking the physical operating system into consideration. The same should be applied on virtualized applications. There are many reasons to use application virtualization. Isolation from the underlying operating system is one of them. If this is your main driver for application virtualization, then there's certainly a point to sandbox as much as possible. But if ease of deployment and updating are your main drivers, then the isolation is not such a big deal.

Often do enterprises have a packaging policy dictating common settings for all packages. Even if your packaging policy specifies a certain location for your sandboxes, for example, the user's roaming profile. Your policy should allow a different location for those few applications that create massive sandboxes and don't need to be roamed.

I'm the first to admit that designing the perfect ThinApp implementation is hard. Because it's perfection we are pursuing, right? At the end of the day, the most important thing is that all decisions are made on the basis of knowledge of the ThinApp technology. Hopefully the rest of the book provides the necessary information for you to make a calculated decision on how your unique implementation will look.

Implementing ThinDirect

Many customers are struggling with a one browser policy. Using one browser that has to support all web applications often means you freeze your browser at a certain version and keep dependencies such as, Java and others, locked down. Updating the browser becomes a huge project that can span for a year (honestly I've seen multiple year long projects). ThinDirect offers you a way out of this hurdle. It's often only a couple of very critical web applications that force you to use a certain version of a browser, having specific settings or being stuck with an outdated dependency. Being able to switch browser on a per web application basis, seamless to the user, is very powerful.

Historically, ThinDirect has been associated quite heavily with virtualizing Internet Explorer 6 (IE6). While this still is a valid use case, I would like to move the focus away from IE6 and different versions of the browser, and focus more on browser settings and different dependencies. If one of your web applications requires a certain setting, why should you apply this setting to all your browsing? Using ThinDirect you can very well have Internet Explorer 8 (IE8) locally installed in a very secure and locked down configuration. When the user needs to access a web application requiring a more unsecure configuration, ThinDirect simply launches a packaged IE8 with the correct configuration. My design proposal is to have the latest and greatest browser, very securely configured together with the latest versions of all dependencies. Then you use ThinApp packaged browsers with ThinDirect to handle the exceptions.

If you are planning on using ThinDirect to offer different settings or dependencies to your users, you should think twice before you actually virtualize the browser. If the correct version is already natively installed, you could use an entry point to launch the locally installed browser but within a new environment instead. This way, you only have one browser instance to maintain and keep updated. You can find out more about about ThinDirect in *Chapter 2*, *Application Packaging* in the section *Virtualizing Internet Explorer 6*.

I would highly recommend that you use **Group Policy Objects** (**GPO**) to manage your ThinDirect implementation. The other method of configuring ThinDirect, using text files, are great for testing, small implementations, and running demos, but do not really fit in a managed enterprise environment. Central management of ThinDirect is much more commonly used and certainly more practical.

Designing for a physical client implementation

The most common deployment scenario for physical clients is local deployment. Most customers use deployment tools such as Microsoft SCCM or similar, and deploy the ThinApp packages as MSIs. You can very well stream to physical devices, but that is mostly used in special use cases. For example, you can choose streaming because of the in-place update mechanism it offers.

Choosing local deployment offers a couple of benefits. It fits seamlessly into the existing processes and the packages have more or less the same performance as a locally installed version of the application.

Where you decide to place your packages on your clients is an interesting discussion. I've seen enterprises creating a specific ThinApp folder on their clients where all ThinApps go. Another method is to deploy the packages into the default location, that is, `C:\Program Files\ApplicationName (VMware ThinApp)`. My personal preference is to deploy packages to `C:\Program Files\ApplicationName`, that is, into the same folder as a natively installed version of the application. I fail to understand why you would feel the need to specify if the application is virtualized by its location, so using the original location seems to be the most logical choice.

The reason for ThinApp to default to an `ApplicationName (VMware ThinApp)` folder name is simply to make sure you do not conflict with a natively installed version. One good side effect when going for the `C:\Program Files\ApplicationName` path is that you'll get rid of the irritating **Side by Side (SxS)** events in the Microsoft Event viewer (for more info, refer to `http://kb.vmware.com/kb/2005254`). These SxS events are purely informational and occur because the Windows operating system can't find the folder that the application appears to be running from.

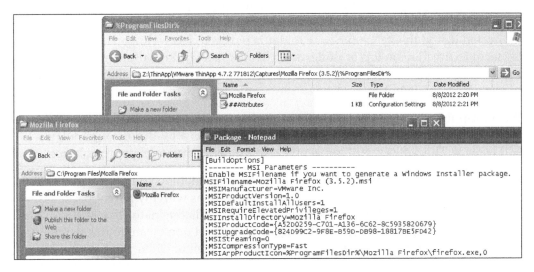

Choosing to deploy the package into the same path as the original application's path is a logical choice. A side effect is you will get rid of most of the SxS events in your event log.

When deploying locally, you need to decide where to place your sandbox. A package that is locally installed can very well use a sandbox located on a network share. If you choose to store the sandbox on a network share, the performance of write and read operations to the sandbox will be limited by the speed of your network and network share. If your package makes minimum use of the sandbox your execution should not be influenced so much. And the other way round, if your package makes much use of the sandbox your users will probably notice a decrease in performance of the application.

Storing the sandbox locally will offer a better application performance. The sandbox can be roamed using the Windows roaming profile. If you use a profile management tool, make sure the tool is configured to download the sandbox completely (sometimes called pre fetching), or the sandbox risks getting corrupted. Many enterprises use the roaming profile more as a backup solution for user's data/settings rather than for offering their users a personalized desktop on different devices. If this is the main reason to use roaming profiles, I instead recommend using a proper backup tool. Backup tools are generally more suitable for pure backup tasks. ThinApp supports redirecting folders, but if you redirect too heavily you can see some side effects. If your packages use `%AppData%` to store the sandbox but you redirected it, and the `My Documents` folder is redirected as well, you have multiple layers of redirection on top or underneath ThinApp's virtualization layer. If your user profile design requires folder redirections you need to verify that the design works with your ThinApp packages.

If your sandboxes are located on a network share, there can be no firewalls between your clients and the share. Even if the firewall supports a 1 GBps throughput, it will add latency. This latency will impact the overall performance of your packages.

If you deploy your packages locally, you will probably deploy your AppLinks locally as well. I don't necessarily use the same path standard as with my parent packages. The reason is that I am much more likely to have a conflicting natively installed runtime. Since AppLinks often are packaged runtimes, I don't want to risk deploying a package into the folder used by a natively installed version. Often you have the latest and greatest runtime natively installed on your clients and use ThinApp to package the odd versions. But I don't separate them into a specific AppLink folder either, for example, `C:\AppLinks`. I prefer to keep my AppLinks in the `C:\Program Files` folder. I often use the default `ApplicationName` (VMware ThinApp) folder name to make sure I use a unique folder. When I build my parent package, I need to know the path to my AppLinks, so having a good naming convention and process in place is a must. An interesting alternative for deploying your parent package and child package in one and the same MSI file is posted on the ThinApp blog, available at `http://blogs.vmware.com/thinapp/2012/08/deploy-thinapp-and-applink-packages-together.html`. The method could be enhanced with logic to cope with AppLinks already deployed on the client machine but other than that, this is a great concept.

One of the most frequent questions I get is "what should I virtualize?" and "what should my Golden Image include natively?". My view on this is pretty straightforward. An application used by all or most of your users should be natively installed in their latest and greatest version. That goes for Microsoft Office as well as Java. The exceptions are very good candidates for ThinApp. For example, an old Java version or the previous version of Microsoft Office used only by a few. An application that is only used by a small number of users, and all troublesome applications, are good candidates for virtualization. Using this approach and my suggestions for folder structure should get you a long way in your ThinApp design for physical clients.

Designing for a virtual desktop infrastructure (VDI) implementation

Virtual desktops, what a great idea! VDI offers central management of your desktops. On paper, this is a perfect solution. In reality, it's still a great solution but only for certain use cases. Very few enterprises can use VDI for their whole user base, but where it's possible it can be a great solution. The holy grail in VDI is to have only one Golden Image, shared by all users. User-unique changes are stored as **delta changes**. Hardly anyone manages to get down to only one Golden Image. One thing you want to make sure though, is that the application entitlement is not forcing you to manage many different Golden Images.

Furthermore, application entitlement shouldn't change the user-unique delta disk. If you achieve this, you will require much less expensive SAN storage, and by minimizing your SAN investment, your VDI ROI (return on investment) and TCO (total cost of ownership) calculation will become much more appealing. Application virtualization is the only packaging technology that will allow you to deploy applications without changing the disk content. Especially when ThinApp is implemented using a streaming deployment method. Streaming ThinApp packages and storing the sandbox to a network share will require no change on the disk. ThinApp streams to memory only, no disk change is made by the ThinApp runtime. The operating system might cache memory to disk, but this is out of the ThinApp runtime's control and the swap file is often something you can discard anyway.

So with this in mind, streaming is a very common deployment method for VDI implementations. But it's not the only deployment method. Local deployment can very well be used. I would recommend it for global applications, that is, applications put in your Golden Image. ThinApp packages can very much be a part of your Golden Image. Streaming is still my recommendation for applications not used by all users, and therefore is subjective to a user-specific entitlement.

The downside of having something in the Golden Image is that it's harder to manage. Updates to applications often require a recompose of the desktops. It doesn't have to, but in reality other methods can very quickly become over engineered. Streaming has the obvious benefit of not changing the disk footprint, but when you look at updating a streaming package using in-place update, it becomes even more appealing. When it comes to entitlement, my favorite is to call `thinreg.exe` from your login script. If your VDI environment is VMware View, you have built-in ThinApp entitlement capabilities. The View Manager can entitle ThinApp packages on a per pool or desktop basis.

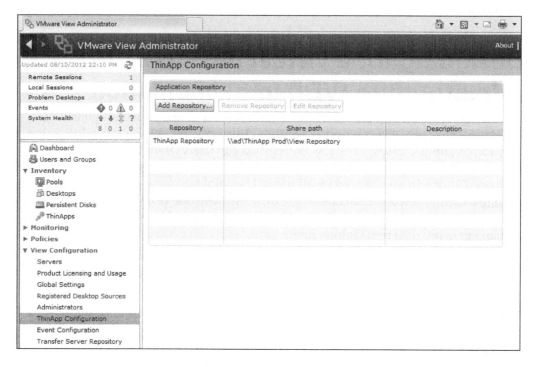

VMware View Manager supports ThinApp entitlement. The previous screenshot shows where you specify one or many ThinApp repositories.

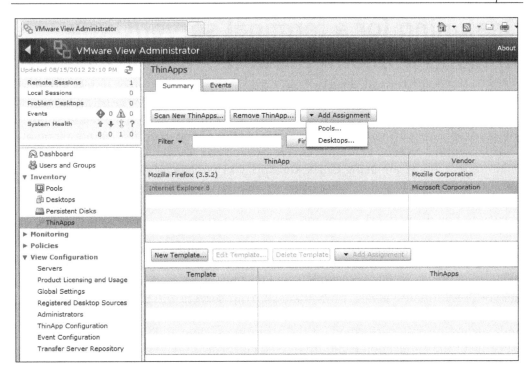

In the View Manager you can assign (entitle) ThinApp packages on a per pool or desktop basis. `thinreg.exe` called from your login script allows you to entitle on a per user basis.

One thing I often come across is a profile management tool being implemented quite heavily in a VDI environment. Very often, the user's folders are being redirected to network shares. It makes a lot of sense to redirect otherwise local folders, because then nothing is stored on the actual virtual desktop. This allows you to use floating pools. Floating pools are when users are not assigned to a specific desktop. All users share the same pool of stateless desktops. ThinApp supports most folder redirections, but I've seen situations where there's too much redirection. Redirection of the user's `%AppData%` (where the sandbox is stored), and redirecting other folders such as `Favorites` or `My Documents`, can become an issue. If you think about it, the write or read operation is going through several redirection layers so it's not surprising if an issue arises. Make sure you test your ThinApp packages in your VDI design to make sure you do not run into any issues.

There are no real changes you need to implement in your packages to support a VDI implementation. When it comes to VDI, my view is very simple. You can't have a good virtual desktop infrastructure without ThinApp.

Designing for a terminal server/Citrix XenApp implementation

Using ThinApp in a terminal server and Citrix environment is more or less identical to running ThinApp in VDI, from a design point of view. The few considerations you have to make for VDI is true for **terminal servers (TS)** as well. One thing that might complicate a TS implementation is the fact that you are often running it on a 64-bit operating system. You may have to tweak your packages to support a 64-bit environment. If you are using Citrix XenApp, you publish a ThinApp package in the same way you would publish any other application on your XenApp server. When you are asked to browse to your application, simply paste the path to your package's entry point on the network share and you're good to go.

I definitely recommend streaming ThinApp packages onto your terminal server/XenApp. In that case, management and support are so much easier. You can place the network share on the same high-speed backbone as your TS environment, so network performance is rarely a bottleneck. Your servers will be more or less clean from application installations, which will make them very stable. Server updates and patches are only performed for the operating system and Citrix components. No patching of the application is required to be performed on your servers. Application updates are handled using the in-place update method. In using streaming, your whole Citrix environment has only one instance of the application. Updating this one single instance will immediately update the application to all your users.

Using ThinApp on Citrix will dramatically lower your *time to market* - no more time consuming manual tweaking in order to get applications installed on each of the servers within a farm. No more time consuming regression tests. Simply verify the functionality of your package, and off you go. `thinreg.exe` in the login script will handle your user entitlement. If you use Active Directory group membership for entitlement, `thinreg.exe` will register, for example, Adobe Reader 8 to one group of users and Adobe Reader X to another. Both groups can be logged in on the same physical terminal server and still have their own file type registrations and their own start menus. `thinreg.exe` registers on a per user basis by default. You should not use the `thinreg.exe/a` switch, which would register machine wide.

Designing for a mixed environment

A mixed environment can be physical clients together with virtual desktops. It can also be a physical and terminal server/Citrix XenApp environments, or any combinations of these. One benefit with ThinApp is the possibility to have one single package supporting all your different environments. The same package can run on physical clients as well as on VDI desktops or Citrix environments. Creating packages supporting many different environments is of course harder than creating a package only supporting one environment.

ThinApp has some parameters you can change dynamically. The ability to change the sandbox location without rebuilding your package is the most useful one. Let's say your physical clients must store the sandbox in the `%AppData%\Thinstall` folder, but your XenApp environment requires the sandboxes to be stored on a network share. In this case you can still create the package with the default location of the sandbox. On your Citrix servers you can specify an environment variable (see in *Chapter 1, Application Virtualiztion*, the section *The sandbox* for more information) overriding the sandbox location. This allows you to have one single package supporting both environments.

You usually have different operating systems types when you have a mixed environment. For example, your terminal servers might run a 64-bit OS while your clients run a 32-bit OS. Some applications have a problem with the change of the `Program Files` folder name on a 64-bit OS. One common workaround is to capture the application being installed into a static path rather than into the dynamic `Program Files` folder. For example, you can install the application into a folder in the root of the C:. This path will be static regardless of whether you use the package on a 32-bit or 64-bit environment.

Another topic on mixed environments is the location of your AppLink packages. Using local deployment of ThinApp packages means that your AppLinks are most likely to be located locally as well. Using a streaming deployment method, typically a VDI/terminal server, your AppLinks are located on a network share. One method supporting both the deployment methods with one package is to use `OptionalAppLinks` pointing to both AppLink locations. You will have to make sure your users on the physical clients can't access the AppLinks located on the network share. This can be achieved with NTFS permissions or firewall rules.

Sizing of your streaming file share

ThinApp streaming is a great method of deployment. It's easy to support since it only requires a standard Windows file server. Your ThinApp packages are easy to maintain using the in-place update. The downside is that it's hard to know how to size your streaming environment. That's because all networks are different, and all packages behave differently when streaming. Two virtualized Microsoft Office 2003 packages can behave very differently from each other. So the only way to efficiently size your streaming implementation is to investigate how your packages behave. That said, the load on the file server is very similar to the load that your normal document file server would bear. There's no difference from a file sharing point of view, if the file is an Excel spreadsheet or a ThinApp package. The file server handles the two types of files identically. If many users request the same package, the file server will probably cache most of the package. Therefore you should size your ThinApp streaming repository just like you would size any other file share. With this in mind I will try to give you a couple of directions that can be helpful when designing your streaming environment.

Your clients must have minimum 100 Mbps LAN access to the ThinApp repository. The connection must be a reliable and a low latency connection. If you would lose connection to the ThinApp repository while running a streamed ThinApp package, it would be the same as losing your hard disk during execution from the application's point of view. No Windows application can cope with that kind of interference, so the packaged application will crash and burn. A low latency connection is important because the default block size when streaming is 64 KB. Many blocks will be transferred to the client when streaming a package. If your network design were to add latency to each block, you can imagine the direct effect on performance. I would recommend using a 1 GB LAN access for best performance.

To be able to correctly size your streaming infrastructure you will need to investigate your packages. You have to measure the amount of data the package will consume when being executed. You can do that using tools such as Wireshark (http://www.wireshark.org). Once you've learned what the package consumes, you need to calculate how many users will launch the package at the same time. If an application consumes 5 MB when launched, and ten users launch the application at the same time, the load on the network will be 50 MB. It's pretty straightforward. If your ThinApp repository contains 10 applications and you have 100 users, not all users will use all 10 ThinApp packages and especially not at the same time. The only way to know the payload on your network and file server is to measure real-life user usage.

There are a couple of things to note when it comes to streaming a package. The first launch of a package will always be slower than the subsequent launches. Upon the first launch the sandbox is initiated, and this will take something like a second or so. Many applications will modify files and registry keys on the first launch, and that may add to the extra long initial launch time. If you launch the application during the capturing process, you'll minimize the amount of changes done during the first launch of the package. There are applications that will open a lot of large files with write permissions upon launch. If these files are located in the virtual environment, then these files will have to be copied into the sandbox when the package launches. The copying operation will be a transfer of data from your ThinApp repository to your sandbox. This behavior will of course greatly affect your launch time. Make sure to investigate the sandbox content during the test run of the package to learn if the package generates a large sandbox. If the package creates a large sandbox upon the first launch, then the package might not be a very good candidate for streaming. Investigate if you can reconfigure the package to better be suitable for streaming.

There are several different ThinApp streaming payloads involved in the streaming process. The first thing that happens during the streaming process is that the ThinApp runtime is downloaded and executed. The ThinApp runtime is about 600 KB in size. After loading the runtime, the sandbox is initiated and the package becomes aware of the virtual environment. If you have AppLink configured, then the AppLink package's environment will be merged into the current environment. This merge is not a copy operation of the entire file content of the AppLink, but rather a copy of the virtual registry. Remember that it's in the virtual registry that the file database is located. This database will tell the runtime where files are located.

Sometimes you'll find AppLink packages demanding that quite a large amount of data is copied into the sandbox. This merged data is located in the sandbox of the parent package in a file called `Merge.`*something*`.tvr`. This file is created or updated on each launch of your package. If the file is large it means that all that data has to be copied on each launch of the package. Since you might have updated your AppLink package since the last launch, the `merge` operation will be made upon each launch of the parent package. There is not much you can do about that other than to make sure that your AppLink packages are as small and clean as possible or simply decide not to AppLink a certain package. The next payload is the launch of the application. If the package is launched for the first time, any first launch modifications will have to be copied to the sandbox. When the application has launched, more data will be downloaded as required by the application. How much will be downloaded depends on the amount that has already been loaded during launching the payload, and the usage of the application. If a user uses a feature in the application that is not already downloaded, the necessary blocks will have to be downloaded.

The sandbox location is of great importance when using a streaming deployment method. If the package is being streamed and the sandbox is located on a network share, you risk hitting the network twice: once for the streaming and again to read/write the sandbox content. Let's say a file located in the virtual environment is opened using the modify permission by the application. The file will first have to be downloaded to the client, and then across the network again to be stored in the sandbox. So in these certain circumstances the network performance will hit your execution twice. If you've decided to store your sandboxes on a network share, I recommend that you store packages and user sandboxes on different file servers. This way you spread the load and don't hit the same server twice during the execution of a package.

When streaming your packages you are very dependent on the availability of the file share. Microsoft DFS is recommended for high availability. DFS also allows you to synchronize your ThinApp repository to branch offices while still maintaining one single namespace. DFS is the preferred method to distribute the ThinApp repository across your organization so that all users have LAN access to the packages. With the help of Active Directory sites your users will always be connected to the closest DFS share.

As you have learned by now, there are quite a lot of things to consider when sizing for a streaming deployment method. Besides ThinApp configurations there are things such as, Server Message Block (SMB) Version 1 and 2 optimizations, that you can apply on your file server and clients to enhance the streaming performance. If you are interested in learning more about tuning SMB please have a look at the following articles:

- MSDN library article:

  Microsoft SMB Protocol and CIFS Protocol Overview

  ```
  http://msdn.microsoft.com/en-us/library/aa365233%28v=vs.85%29.
  aspx
  ```

- Jose Barreto's Blog article

  FSCT test results detail the performance of Windows Server 2008 R2 File Server configurations - 23,000 users with 192 spindles

  ```
  http://blogs.technet.com/b/josebda/archive/2011/04/08/fsct-
  test-results-detail-the-performance-of-windows-server-2008-r2-
  file-server-configurations-23-000-users-with-192-spindles.aspx
  ```

If you have poor initial launch times, the first thing to investigate is the sandbox. If the sandbox is small, bad performance is probably due to services or fonts being initiated during the launch, and not so much the fact you are streaming the package. Another good test procedure is to launch your package locally. Does the ThinApp package launch fast locally but is slow when it's launched as a streamed package? Then the problem has to be network related, or the application is simply not suitable for streaming.

Antivirus software configured to scan your ThinApp repository on access is probably the worst performance killer out there. You must make sure that you disable on-access scanning of your ThinApp packages. No antivirus software I know of knows how to read a ThinApp package anyway, so scanning the packages has no point. Your ThinApp repository should have read and execute permissions only for all your users. Only the administrators should have the modify permission, so turning on the on-access scanning should be safe. And remember, there should be no firewalls between your clients and the ThinApp repository. The latency added by a firewall will make your package's execution extremely slow.

Summary

In this chapter we've looked at some design and implementation considerations. It's a complicated topic, since all environments are different. I hope this chapter has provided you with some more insight into how to go about designing your implementation of ThinApp.

In the next chapter we'll dive into the wonderful world of troubleshooting.

7

Troubleshooting

Not all applications can be successfully virtualized by just clicking on the next button in Setup Capture. Sometimes you'll have to troubleshoot an application in order to get it virtualized. In this chapter I'll cover the basics of troubleshooting ThinApp packages. Unfortunately there is no such thing as a silver bullet when it comes to troubleshooting. There is no single easy fix to all packaging issues. All applications are different so each package must be handled separately. In this chapter, we will look at the following topics:

- Troubleshooting theory
- Effective test procedures
- Common tools used for troubleshooting
- ThinApp Log Monitor
- Troubleshooting tips and tricks
- Your typical every day capturing process

The theory behind troubleshooting

The theory behind troubleshooting looks the same no matter what you are troubleshooting. In order to be successful in your troubleshooting, you must have a structured method. The method looks like this:

1. Gather data about the issue.
2. Create a hypothesis, with the help of the collected data, about what will solve the issue.
3. Verify if the hypothesis is true or not.
4. If the hypothesis is true, go to step 8.

5. If the hypothesis is wrong, do some more data collection.

6. Create a new hypothesis.

7. Verify if the hypothesis is true or not (do step 5 through 7 until you find that your hypothesis is true).

8. Since you figured out what the root cause is, you either can or cannot solve the issue. If the issue is something you can solve, implement the solution and the issue is resolved.

Pretty basic stuff. This method can be used on anything that needs to be fixed. I used to work as a sound technician before I entered the world of computers and I used this process for troubleshooting issues with my sound system. Today, working as a ThinApp packager, I use it to troubleshoot packages that are not running.

As I see it, there are three major ingredients involved in troubleshooting, which are as follows:

- Data collection
- Test procedure
- Knowledge in the topic of troubleshooting

You will spend a lot of time gathering data. You will process this data using your experience and knowledge in the subject. Since you will probably have to verify many different hypotheses (you hardly ever get it right the first time), your test process must be very efficient. If all three ingredients are in place, you'll manage to troubleshoot pretty much anything they throw at you. Hopefully you have gained knowledge in ThinApp by now, reading this book. Experience can only be gained by getting your hands dirty. You need to package quite a few applications with ThinApp before you get the hang of it. In the following sections of this chapter I'll talk about different data gathering tools and techniques as well as how to form an efficient test process.

When troubleshooting, it's hard to know where to start. You are faced with too many variables. Is it something within the application? Is it something concerning the ThinApp runtime? Or can it be the operating system? When doing troubleshooting it's important to minimize the variables. Being stuck with too many variables leaves you to rely on pure luck while trying to find the root cause of the issue. We must take the guesswork out of troubleshooting.

Effective test procedures

It's all about your test procedures. The first test procedure I'll explain targets minimizing the number of variables you're facing, helping you to focus on what is most likely the cause of the issue. The VMware ThinApp blog (`https://blogs.vmware.com/thinapp/2010/10/thinapp-troubleshooting-methods.html`) discusses the test procedure, consisting of four steps, for minimizing the variables. The four steps should be conducted in a sequence. If one test step fails, there's no point conducting a new test step because the next one will fail as well. Stop at the failing test step and try to solve why the package is failing before moving on.

The test procedure should be used when there's an issue with a package. You're not supposed to run through all the four steps with all your packages.

Let's have a closer look at each step.

The Dirty Test

The Dirty Test means that when you have just finished the capture process, while the captured application is still locally installed on your capturing machine, you launch the newly compiled package. A package rarely fails to launch during the Dirty Test, because the application is locally installed. If the package fails, it's most likely due to one of two reasons. One being that there's something wrong with the entry point. Things to look at first are the `Source`, `WorkingDirectory` or `CommandLine` parameters. The second possible reason for it to fail is that the ThinApp runtime has an issue running this application. If this is the case, it suddenly becomes extremely complicated. While there may be workarounds, such as loading components outside of the virtual environment, the VMware ThinApp developers quite often need to have a look at the issue. To get help from VMware you must file a support ticket. Filing a support ticket often involves uploading logfiles, the project folder, and original installation media. Basically, what is required is a method of reproducing the issue. If not reproducible in any other way you need to allow remote troubleshooting if you want to have the issue looked at.

The Washed Test

The next step in your test procedure is the Washed Test. The Washed Test still uses your capturing environment with the application locally installed, but this time you go into the **Add or Remove Programs** control panel and uninstall the application. Once it's uninstalled, you test run your package. As we all know, an uninstallation will most likely leave components behind. If the application you captured consists of multiple components, uninstall one at a time and test the package after each component uninstallation. Let's say you captured application A together with its dependency Java 1.6.26. Uninstall Java, and if the package still functions you can go ahead and uninstall application A. If the package now fails you can be pretty certain the issue is not the virtualization of Java. It has to be related to the components of application A. Now, you can focus on the application A, and discard anything related to Java. This way you've managed to minimize the variables.

The Clean Test

If the Dirty Test and Washed Test are both successful, it's time for the Clean Test. When doing the Clean Test, it's crucial not to introduce any new variables. You should run the test on a clean instance of your capturing environment. Simply revert your capturing virtual machine to the snapshot used when starting your capturing process. If the package fails during this test it indicates that there are components installed by the application that are not captured in the virtual environment. Most of the time you can notice this during the Washed Test. But since the uninstallation of an application hardly ever uninstalls everything completely, the Clean Test is still very important. Another important reason to conduct the Clean Test is to make sure that the application can be packaged using ThinApp. If your ThinApp package runs on a clean machine, you know the application works within the virtualized environment of ThinApp. You can therefore discard the ThinApp runtime as the root cause to why the application isn't running as expected in your production environment.

The Production Test

Our last test is to run the package on a production environment. Your production environment may consist of many different operating systems and platforms. You must verify the package on all systems. If the package fails during this phase it must be due to some environmental issue. The Clean Test proved that the package is working, so the source of the issue must be located outside of the package. With that being said, the fix might very well be to change the configuration of the package.

Try to limit all variables normally found on the production environment. Limit the amount of locally installed applications. Minimize group policies applied to the client. Hopefully these steps will give you a general idea about where the issue resides. If your production environment is a different operating system, try capturing the application on the same operating system. If possible, install the application natively. This might provide some more data for you to process during the troubleshooting process.

After you've gathered data and limited the variables using the previous test procedures, you have hopefully come up with a hypothesis. It's now time to test your hypothesis, proving whether or not it is true. I prefer to run as many tests as possible within the virtual environment. This way, I'll learn immediately if my hypothesis is true or not. Since all changes are located in the sandbox, it will be easy to revert my testing by simply deleting the sandbox. If I manage to figure out a fix, I can very easily merge my modified sandbox into the project folder using `sbmerge.exe`. Since I don't have to rebuild the project folder for each test, I will save a lot of time. Not all modifications can be applied using this method. For example, there is no easy method of changing the isolation mode on the fly. Changing many `Package.ini` files and isolation modes will force you to rebuild your whole project folder. Typical tools to use when modifying the running virtual environment are entry points to `cmd.exe` and `regedit.exe`. With these I can place myself inside the virtual environment and copy files, change registry keys, and do whatever else my hypothesis dictates. Limit the amount of changes you apply between test runs. You do not want to change too much or you may end up fixing the first issue but adding a second issue.

Let's have a look at a very simple example of packaged Microsoft Project 2003 giving an MSI error when launched on a Windows 7, 64-bit operating system. The application was captured using a Windows XP, 32-bit environment:

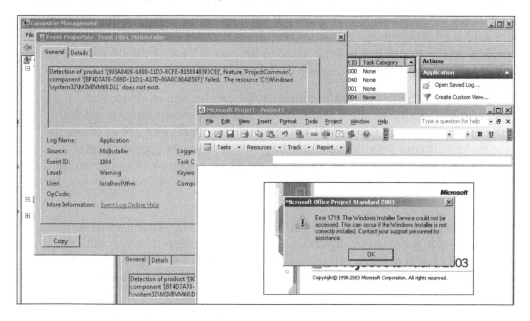

MS Project 2003 gives you an MSI self repair issue when running on Windows 7.

The MSI self repair is due to `msvbvm60.dll` being missing or, in this case, actually being available but in the wrong version.

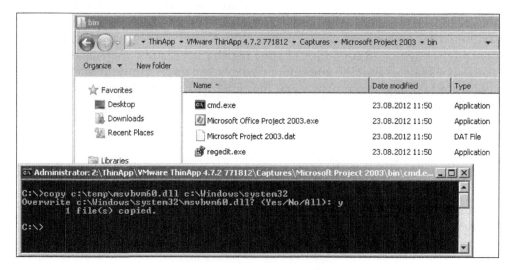

My MS Project 2003 package has entry points for `regedit.exe` and `cmd.exe`.

Launching the `cmd.exe` entry point allows me to copy an older version of `msvbvm60.dll`, replacing the newer one available in Windows 7. The change is only affecting my virtual environment. Modifications are stored in the sandbox.

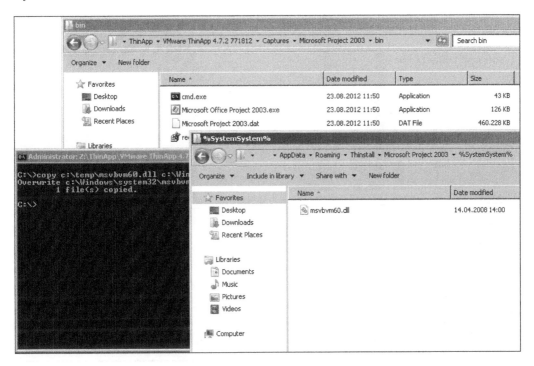

The file I copied using the `cmd.exe` entry point will end up in the sandbox.

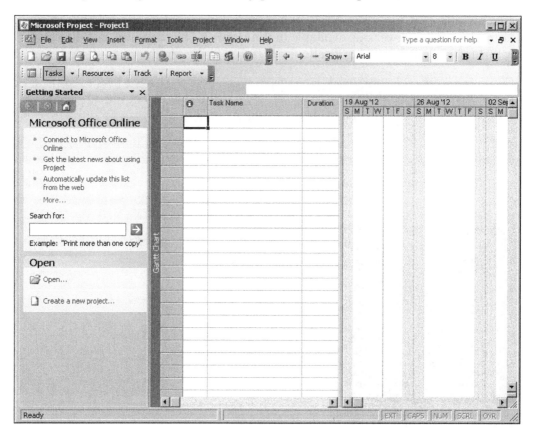

Once the correct version of `msvbvm60.dll` has been copied into the correct location, I can exit the `cmd.exe` and immediately verify if the issue was fixed by launching Microsoft Project. MS Project launches without starting any MSI self-repairs. No rebuilding of my project folder was necessary.

To implement this fix into your project, simply run `sbmerge.exe` and rebuild the project folder. For this method of applying changes to the current virtual environment to work the best, you should make sure that your package uses WriteCopy as the default directory isolation mode. You never know where you'll be doing changes, so it would be safest to sandbox everything.

Common troubleshooting tools

The tools you use for troubleshooting are often referred to as troubleshooting tools. I prefer to call them data collecting tools. I've yet to see a troubleshooting tool that presents me with a dialog box, and tells me what the root cause of the issue is. All tools used to troubleshoot are tools that provide you with as much data as possible. Using your experience and knowledge, you filter through the data and can hopefully find the root cause of the issue. When you turn to these data collecting tools you'll spend a significant amount of time digesting all the data.

Whatever tool you are accustomed to using when packaging a traditional MSI package, should and can be used for troubleshooting ThinApp packages. Here's a list of common tools that I use. You may have others and you should be able to continue using those.

Process Explorer

Process Explorer from **Sysinternals**, now owned by Microsoft, is a great tool for finding out what is running on your machine. It is free and available here: `http://technet.microsoft.com/en-us/sysinternals/bb896653`.

Troubleshooting with the help of **Process Explorer** often means I run it on two machines, one where the application is natively installed and one where I run my packaged version. Then I compare the process list and look for differences. Please notice that it may be easier if your package is configured using `ProcessExternalNameBehavior=Original`.

If something is keeping your sandbox locked and you need to find out what process it is, **Process Explorer** is perfect. Run **Process Explorer** and search for .rw (part of the name of the registry files within the sandbox). Whatever is accessing the .rw files is what's keeping your sandbox from not closing cleanly.

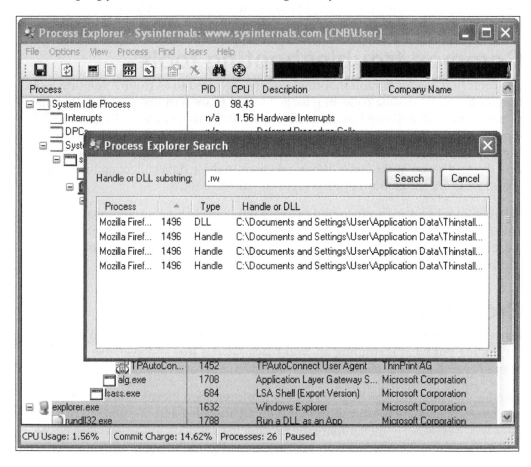

Searching for `.rw` will show you what's keeping the sandbox opened.

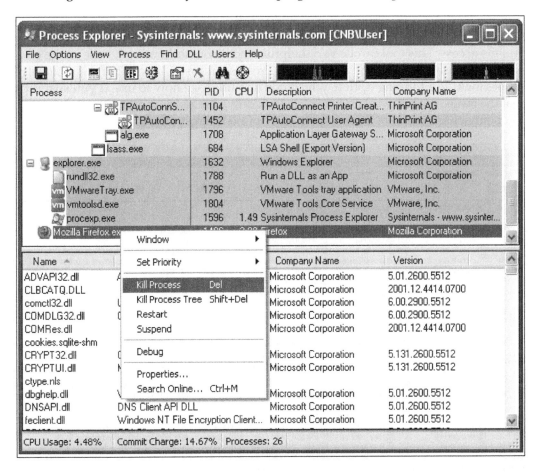

Double-clicking on the process name in the search result will take you to the process and then you can kill it.

Things keeping the sandbox from closing down are often services that are not shutting down, or if the application is a Microsoft one it's often due to `ctfmon.exe` or `mdm.exe` running.

Process Monitor

Process Monitor is yet another tool from **Sysinternals,** http://technet.
microsoft.com/en-us/sysinternals/bb896645. This tool shows you all registry
and file access. This tool can be very helpful when troubleshooting a wide range of
issues. The problem with the tool is that it creates a massive amount of data. Luckily
it does include a filtering option, which you should learn how to use. If you suspect
that the issue is registry related you can look only at registry access. You can also
filter out actions made by processes that are of no interest to your troubleshooting.

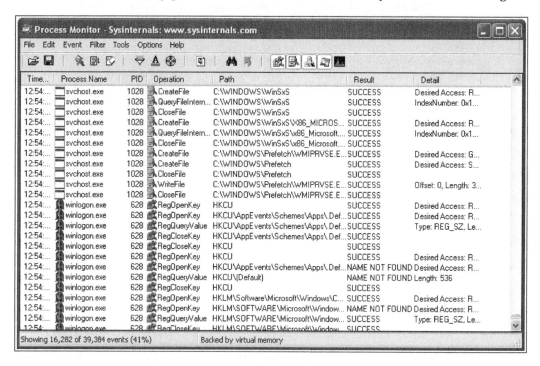

The previous image shows **Process Monitor** in action.

I always run **Process Monitor** natively, outside the virtual environment. **Process
Monitor** uses a device driver, which can't be launched by the ThinApp runtime.

Dependency Walker

Dependency Walker is another great tool. It can be downloaded from here:
`http://www.dependencywalker.com`. **Dependency Walker** will show you any
missing dependencies an application may have on a system. It can be launched either
from inside the virtual bubble, with the help of a `cmd.exe` entry point, or launched
outside. It's important not to run **Dependency Walker** on the package, that is, one
of the entry points. **Dependency Walker** should investigate the dependencies of the
application's original `.exe` file and not the dependencies of ThinApp runtime. You
will always get at least a couple of false positives running **Dependency Walker**.
Search the web for more information about the missing dependencies and you'll
soon learn which ones you can discard.

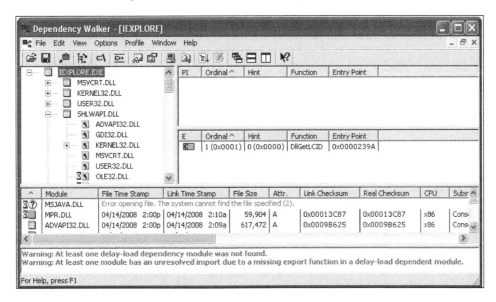

Here's a test of the natively installed `iexplore.exe`. Two files are reported as
having issues. This is normal and you'll soon learn which errors to discard.

Dependency Walker is a very powerful tool when troubleshooting Windows XP
legacy applications and why they do not run on Windows 7.

Microsoft Event Viewer

Don't forget about the Event Viewer. Sometimes the issue is reported in the Event Log.
Although, SxS error can be discarded most of the time. Most SxS issues occur because
the operating system cannot find the path reported by the application. Simply create
the application's original folder in Program Files and the SxS events go away.

Error messages

Sometimes, you get an error message from the application. Read what it says! It can often be valuable information for your troubleshooting.

ThinApp Log Monitor

The ThinApp Log Monitor is a great log tool. It's great because it captures everything that happens within the virtual environment. That being said, it's close to impossible to find the issue because of all of the data it provides. I must be honest; I rarely use the ThinApp Log Monitor. It is my last resort when no other troubleshooting tool gives me any valuable data. You will often find ThinApp Log Monitor logs of 2GB or more, and that is in a clear text format. You can imagine the massive amounts of data contained in each of these files.

ThinApp Log Monitor can be found in the ThinApp utilities folder. You need to launch Log Monitor prior to launching the package for logging to start. Let's create a log using Log Monitor:

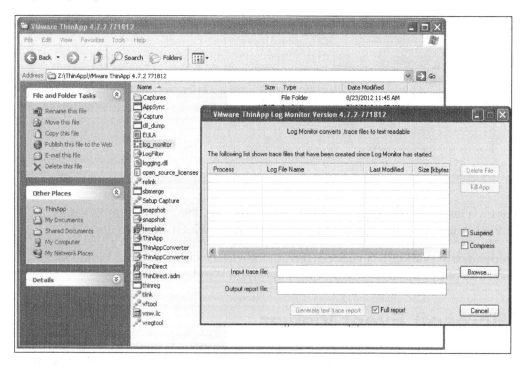

Start by launching **log_monitor.exe** found in the ThinApp utilities folder.

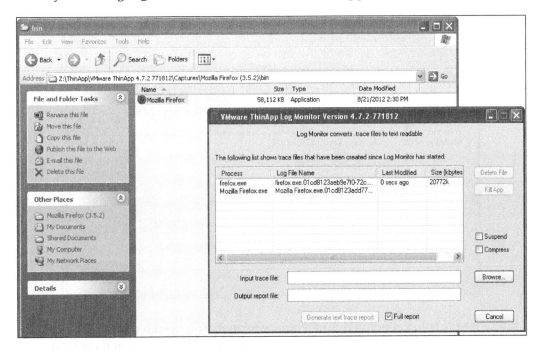

Next, navigate to your package and launch it. You will notice that the log is being generated immediately. When the package is hosted on a network share, you will see at least two processes listed. Only one is the actual execution of the application. The biggest one is normally the log you want.

You will also notice that the performance of the package becomes much slower than normal. Running Log Monitor is very resource intensive.

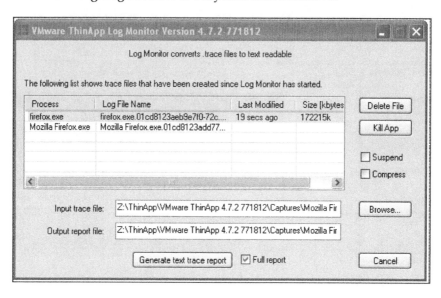

The log that is being generated is in a binary format. You need to convert it into a text file in order to be able to read it. Click on the trace of interest and click on **Generate text trace report**.

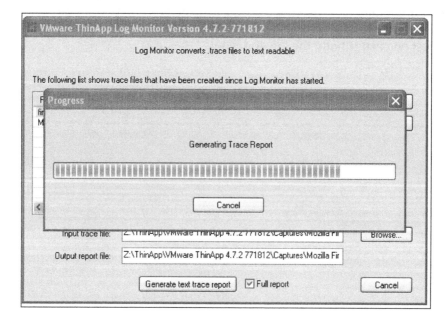

Generating the text version of the logfile is often a time consuming process.

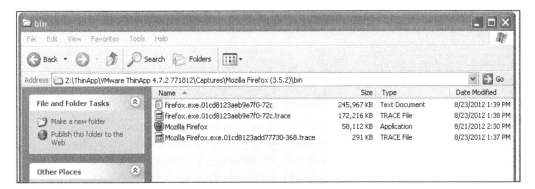

Once the text file is generated you will find it next to the package files together with the binary versions. Once converted to text, you can safely delete the binary versions. You will not need them anymore.

Opening up the logfiles shows the massive amount of data available to you.

You shouldn't use `Notepad.exe` to investigate the logfiles. Notepad can't handle large text files. My personal favorites are TextPad (`http://www.textpad.com`) on Windows and TextWrangler (`http://www.barebones.com/products/TextWrangler`) on MacOS. Both are capable of handling really large text files and have the option to color code the text for easier reading.

You should use the same version of Log Monitor as the one that your ThinApp package is compiled with. If you need to figure out which version of ThinApp runtime your package has, simply launch the package with the **–ThinstallVersion** switch.

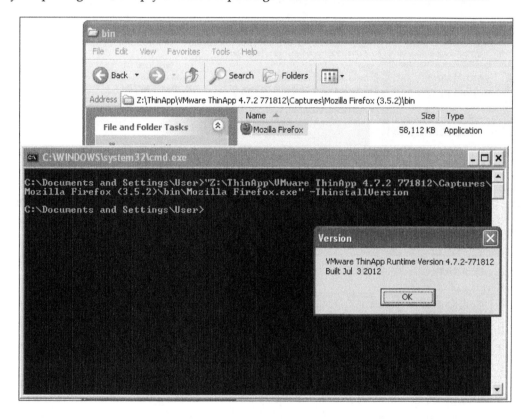

Launching a package with the **–ThinstallVersion** switch will provide you with the ThinApp runtime of the package.

Believe it or not, there's a structure to the logfile that the Log Monitor creates. Your starting point should be the end of the logfile where you'll find the **Potential Errors Detected** section. Here, all the log entries with possible issues are listed. Sometimes you find missing dlls or registry keys reported. If you encounter a log entry of interest, you can search for the log entry ID (the first number on each row) to find the original location in the logfile and investigate what happened before the error and thereby hopefully figure out the root cause. Errors identified by Log Monitor will be marked with * * * for easier identification. You will probably never see a logfile without any entries in the **Potential Errors Detected** section. The execution could be checking for a registry key that is not there. An error would be registered but the application might not really care and happily continue executing. Exceptions and MSI errors are of extra interest if they are found in this section.

The first section of the Log Monitor lists some environmental information about the client where you captured the log.

The vast majority of the logfile contains the API section. Here you can see all the API calls with any of the parameters used, such as input parameters, output parameters, exit records, and more. ThinApp runtime logs runtime messages as well. An API log entry looks something like this:

```
947264 072c 05d8 MOZCRT19.dll:781399b2->kernel32.dll:7c8097d0
TlsGetValue (DWORD dwTlsIndex=16h)
```

Here, `947264` is the event ID, `MOZCRT19.dll` is source dll making the API call, `->` indicates the direction of the API call, `<-` indicates a response, and `kernel32.dll` is the destination dll.

Here's an output from a trace I did a while ago. This was a Windows XP legacy application not executing on Windows 7. The real application name has been changed. Here, the issue is presented to you in clear text:

Log Monitor trace:

```
048200 00000000 00000a00    Can't load library MSVCP50.dll which is
implicitly loaded by C:\Application A\DLLIAP.dll, err=53

049742 00000000 00000a00    Can't load library DLLIAP.dll which is
implicitly loaded by C:\Application A\Application A.exe, err=53
```

Solution:

In this case, the solution was simply to copy `MSVCP50.dll` into the `%SystemSystem%` folder and rebuild the project.

Troubleshooting tips and tricks

Here are a couple of tips and tricks regarding troubleshooting. Just some shortcuts that have helped me out a few times:

- Launch the application from within a `CMD.EXE` entry point: One troubleshooting method is to have the application locally installed and launch the application from within a `CMD.EXE` entry point of an empty project. You can create an empty project by simply running Setup Capture and step through the wizard without altering your capturing environment at all. If you fail to launch the natively installed application by using this empty package's `CMD.EXE` entry point, this may indicate that ThinApp runtime can't execute the application.

- Move suspected files into the support folder: If the package crashes, it's sometimes due to the fact that captured DLLs are not able to run on a certain operating system. One of the first things that I would try when facing this issue is to move the content of `%SystemRoot%` and `%SystemSystem%` into the `support` folder, found in the project folder, and rebuild. This will exclude the files from being a part of the package's virtual environment. If the package behaves differently, I add groups of the moved content back into the original folder macro (bringing them back into the virtual environment). I rebuild and test run the package between each modification. Hopefully I'm able to find the DLL that is causing the issue. I use the same process, moving content to the support folder, when I clean up my project folder. This way, if I get a little overeager, I can revert my modifications.

- Launch the application from a `CMD.EXE` entry point of the package: I use this method to verify if I have an entry point issue or not. This is a different procedure than the first bullet point. Here, the `CMD.EXE` entry point is running within the same virtual environment as the packaged application. The test looks like this:

  1. Launch the `CMD.EXE` entry point.
  2. Navigate to the folder where the executable is, for example, `C:\Program Files\Mozilla Firefox`.
  3. Launch the application, for example, run `firefox.exe`.

  If the application now launches successfully, it indicates that something is wrong with the entry point. The first things to investigate are `WorkingDirectory` and `CommandLine` parameters.

- Register the package: Sometimes, you have to register the package for it to be fully functional. Simply run `thinreg.exe` to register the package on your test machine. You don't have to create an MSI file just in order to register the package. Running `thinreg.exe` will be enough.

- Change the process name behavior: Some applications get confused when they can't find its processes listed in the Task Manager as running. By default, ThinApp packages hide the original process names. Try adding `ProcessExternalNameBehavior=Original` to your `Package.ini` and the original process names will be listed.

- Common DLL often needed when migrating Windows XP applications to Windows 7: If you are migrating a legacy Windows XP application to Windows 7, there are a few DLLs that often need to be included in the package. These DLLs are shared resources, such as libraries. Try adding one or a few of the following DLLs from Windows XP to your project folder and the `%SystemSystem%` folder macro:

```
MFCxx.DLL

MFCxxU.DLL

MSVBMxx.DLL

MSVCRT.DLL

MSVCRT20.DLL

MSVCRT40.DLL

MSVCPxx.DLL

COMADDIN.DLL

COMCAT.DLL

COMCTL32.DLL

COMDLG32.DLL

COMMDLG.DLL
```

xx are to be replaced with numbers, for example, 40, 42, 50 or 60.

Your everyday capturing process

My suggestion, when it comes to how your everyday capturing process should look, is to not run all four test steps in the test procedure discussed in the *Effective test procedures* section. As most of your packages will run just fine, always running all the test steps is not needed. Your capturing process should support troubleshooting if needed but be as efficient as possible.

Your typical capturing process is as follows:

1. Capture the application.
2. Perform the Dirty Test.
    1. Running the Dirty Test will verify if the application can run virtualized at all.
    2. Investigate the sandbox (get to know the application).
    3. Delete the sandbox; this will show if any processes are being left behind running.
3. If the previous steps are successful, do a snapshot of your virtual machine (you might need to return to it for performing the Washed Test).
4. Conduct a Production environment Test.
    1. On failure, go back to the snapshot created in step 3 and run the Washed and Clean tests.

Summary

In this chapter you have learned about some basic ThinApp troubleshooting methods and tools. Troubleshooting is often hard. But the more you practice the easier it becomes. The hardest part is to get the time needed to conduct successful troubleshooting. Your first troubleshooting session will probably take a long time. But after a while you will find that troubleshooting becomes easier and quicker.

Next, you'll find *References* covering the `Packaging.ini` parameters and the physical locations of all folder macros.

References

Folder macros

The following table shows the supported folder macros in ThinApp 4.7.2, and their locations. Windows XP, Windows Server 2003 R2, and older operating systems are considered legacy versions, while Microsoft Vista, Windows Server 2008, and the later versions are listed as modern versions of Windows in the following table:

Macro name	Legacy Windows location	Modern Windows location
`%Drive_C%`	`C:\`	`C:\`
`%Profiles%`	`C:\Documents and Settings\`	`C:\Users`
`%Profile%`	`C:\Documents and Settings\Username\`	`C:\Users\Username\`
`%AppData%`	`C:\Documents and Settings\Username\Application Data\`	`C:\Users\Username\AppData\Roaming\`
`%Cookies%`	`C:\Documents and Settings\Username\Cookies\`	`C:\Users\Username\AppData\Roaming\Microsoft\Windows\Cookies\`
`%Desktop%`	`C:\Documents and Settings\Username\Desktop\`	`C:\Users\Username\Desktop\`
`%Favorites%`	`C:\Documents and Settings\Username\Favorites\`	`C:\Users\Username\Favorites\`

Macro name	Legacy Windows location	Modern Windows location
`%Local AppData%`	`C:\Documents and Settings\Username\ Local Settings\ Application Data\`	`C:\Users\Username\ AppData\Local\`
`%CDBurnArea%`	`C:\Documents and Settings\Username\ Local Settings\ Application Data\ Microsoft\CD Burning\`	`C:\Users\Username\ AppData\Local\Microsoft\ Windows\Burn\`
`%History%`	`C:\Documents and Settings\Username\ Local Settings\ History\`	`C:\Users\Username\ AppData\Local\Microsoft\ Windows\History\`
`%TEMP%`	`C:\Documents and Settings\Username\ Local Settings\Temp\`	`C:\Users\Username\ AppData\Local\Temp\`
`%Internet Cache%`	`C:\Documents and Settings\Username\ Local Settings\ Temporary Internet Files\`	`C:\Users\Username\ AppData\Local\Microsoft\ Windows\Temporary Internet Files\`
`%Personal%`	`C:\Documents and Settings\Username\My Documents\`	`C:\Users\Username\ Documents\`
`%Recent%`	`C:\Documents and Settings\Username\My Recent Documents\`	`C:\Users\Username\ AppData\Roaming\ Microsoft\Windows\Recent\`
`%NetHood%`	`C:\Documents and Settings\Username\ NetHood\`	`C:\Users\Username\ AppData\Roaming\ Microsoft\Windows\Network Shortcuts\`
`%PrintHood%`	`C:\Documents and Settings\Username\ PrintHood\`	`C:\Users\Username\ AppData\Roaming\ Microsoft\Windows\Printer Shortcuts\`
`%SendTo%`	`C:\Documents and Settings\Username\ SendTo\`	`C:\Users\Username\ AppData\Roaming\ Microsoft\Windows\SendTo\`
`%Programs%`	`C:\Documents and Settings\Username\ Start Menu\Programs\`	`C:\Users\Username\ AppData\Roaming\ Microsoft\Windows\Start Menu\Programs\`

Macro name	Legacy Windows location	Modern Windows location
%AdminTools%	C:\Documents and Settings\Username\Start Menu\Programs\Administrative Tools\	C:\Users\Username\AppData\Roaming\Microsoft\Windows\Start Menu\Programs\Administrative Tools\
%Startup%	C:\Documents and Settings\Username\Start Menu\Programs\Startup\	C:\Users\Username\AppData\Roaming\Microsoft\Windows\Start Menu\Programs\Startup\
%Templates%	C:\Documents and Settings\Username\Templates\	C:\Users\Username\AppData\Roaming\Microsoft\Windows\Templates\
%Common AppData%	C:\Documents and Settings\All Users\Application Data\	C:\ProgramData\
%Common Desktop%	C:\Documents and Settings\All Users\Desktop\	C:\Users\Public\Desktop\
%Common Documents%	C:\Documents and Settings\All Users\Documents\	C:\Users\Public\Documents\
%Common Favorites%	C:\Documents and Settings\All Users\Favorites\	C:\Users\Username\Favorites
%Common StartMenu%	C:\Documents and Settings\All Users\Start Menu\	C:\ProgramData\Microsoft\Windows\Start Menu\
%Common Programs%	C:\Documents and Settings\All Users\Start Menu\Programs\	C:\ProgramData\Microsoft\Windows\Start Menu\Programs\
%Common AdminTools%	C:\Documents and Settings\All Users\Start Menu\Programs\Administrative Tools\	C:\ProgramData\Microsoft\Windows\Start Menu\Programs\Administrative Tools\
%Common Startup%	C:\Documents and Settings\All Users\Start Menu\Programs\Startup\	C:\ProgramData\Microsoft\Windows\Start Menu\Programs\Startup\
%Common Templates%	C:\Documents and Settings\All Users\Templates\	C:\ProgramData\Microsoft\Windows\Templates\

Macro name	Legacy Windows location	Modern Windows location
%ProgramFilesDir%	C:\Program Files\ or C:\Program Files (x86)\	C:\Program Files\ or C:\Program Files (x86)\
%Program Files Common%	C:\Program Files\Common Files\	C:\Program Files\Common Files\ or C:\Program Files (x86)\Common Files\
%SystemRoot%	C:\Windows\	C:\Windows\
%Fonts%	C:\Windows\Fonts\	C:\Windows\Fonts\
%Resources%	C:\Windows\Resources\	C:\Windows\Resources\
%Resources Localized%	C:\Windows\Resources\<language_ID>\	C:\Windows\Resources\<language_ID>
%SystemSystem%	C:\Windows\System32\ or C:\Windows\SysWOW64\	C:\Windows\System32\ or C:\Windows\SysWOW64\
%Drive_M%	M:\	M:\

Package.ini parameters

The list of all known `Package.ini` settings are listed in this section. The *ThinApp Package.ini Parameters Reference Guide* (`http://www.vmware.com/pdf/thinapp47_packageini_reference.pdf`) offers even more detail on most of the parameters.

Since Version 4.7.2 of ThinApp, all `Package.ini` settings are case insensitive. If you're using a version prior to 4.7.2, I recommend that you consider all parameters to be case sensitive.

- `AccessDeniedMsg`: A message is displayed to the user if they're not entitled to use the package. This works hand-in-hand with `PermittedGroups`.

  Example:

  ```
  [BuildOptions]
  AccessDeniedMsg=You do not have permission to use this
  application.
  ```

- `AddPageExecutePermission`: The `AddPageExecutePermission` parameter allows legacy applications that don't support a DEP-protected environment, to execute on DEP-enabled operating systems such as Windows XP SP2 and the later versions.

Example:

```
[BuildOptions]
AddPageExecutionPermission=1 (default 0)
```

- `AllowExternalKernelModeServices`: ThinApp runtime can start external kernel driver services as long as the file exists on the physical filesystem. The default setting is not to allow ThinApp runtime to launch these external services.

Example:

```
[BuildOptions]
AllowExternalKernelModeServices=1 (default=0)
```

- `AllowExternalProcessModifications`: Using the `AllowExternalProcessModifications` parameter, you can allow the ThinApp runtime to create and run kernel driver services. The service executable file must exist on the physical filesystem.

Example:

```
[BuildOptions]
AllowExternalProcessModifications=1 (default 0)
```

- `AllowUnsupportedExternalChildProcesses`: ThinApp runtime does not support running 64-bit child processes within the virtual environment. Therefore, ThinApp will by default execute 64-bit child processes outside of the virtualized environment. You can disable this with `AllowUnsupportedExternalChildProcesses`. When it's disabled, no 64-bit child processes will be able to run.

Example:

```
[BuildOptions]
AllowUnsupportedExternalChildProcesses=0 (default 1)
```

- `AnsiCodePage`: This parameter gets its value from the capturing machine. It represents the language (in a numeric format) of your capturing machine. This parameter doesn't allow for language translations.

Example:

```
[BuildOptions]
AnsiCodePage=1252
```

- `AppSyncClearSandboxOnUpdate`: `AppSyncClearSandboxOnUpdate` will delete the sandbox upon a successful AppSync update. The default behavior is to not delete the sandbox.

  Example:

  ```
  [BuildOptions]
  AppSyncClearSandboxOnUpdate=1 (default=0)
  ```

- `AppSyncExpireMessage`: A message is displayed to the user when a package has expired using the `AppSyncExpirePeriod` parameter.

  Example:

  ```
  [BuildOptions]
  AppSyncExpireMessage=This application has been unable to contact
  its update server for %expire_days% day(s), so it is unavailable
  for use. Check your network connection and try again.
  ```

- `AppSyncExpirePeriod`: `AppSyncExpirePeriod` specifies if the package should expire after a certain amount of days of not being able to contact the specified `AppSyncURL`.

  Example:

  ```
  [BuildOptions]
  AppSyncExpirePeriod=30 (AppSyncExpirePeriod=never disables
  expiration of the Package)
  ```

- `AppSyncUpdatedMessage`: A message is displayed to the user after a successful AppSync update.

  Example:

  ```
  [BuildOptions]
  AppSyncUpdatedMessage=Your application have now been updated to
  the latest version.
  ```

- `AppSyncUpdateFrequency`: The `AppSyncUpdateFrequency` parameter decides how often AppSync should check for an updated version of the package. Remember that AppSync will only happen when the package is in use.

  Example:

  ```
  [BuildOptions]
  AppSyncUpdateFrequency=0 (AppSync will check for updates every
  time the Package is launched,default value is 1d)
  ```

- `AppSyncURL`: The `AppSyncURL` parameter specifies the location of update packages, using the AppSync update feature. `AppSyncURL` supports three protocols—HTTP, HTTPS, and FILE.

  Example:

  ```
  [BuildOptions]
  AppSyncURL=file://ServerName/ShareName/NewPackage.exe
  or
  AppSyncURL=http://www.myUpdates.com/Updates/NewPackage.exe
  ```

- `AppSyncWarningFrequency`: This parameter specifies how often the `AppSyncWarningFrequency` value will be displayed, ahead of the expiration of the package.

  Example:

  ```
  [BuildOptions]
  AppSyncWarningFrequency=1d
  ```

- `AppSyncWarningMessage`: This parameter specifies the message displayed to the user before the package expires due to the `AppSyncExpirePeriod` parameter.

  Example:

  ```
  [BuildOptions]
  AppSyncWarningMessage=This application will become unavailable
  for use in %remaining_days% day(s) if it cannot contact its update
  server. Check your network connection to ensure uninterrupted
  service.
  ```

- `AppSyncWarningPeriod`: The parameter specifies how many days ahead of package expiration the `AppSyncWarningMessage` string will start to be displayed. The frequency of the message is decided using the `AppSyncWarningFrequency` parameter.

  Example:

  ```
  [BuildOptions]
  AppSyncWarningPeriod=5d
  ```

- `AutoShutdownServices`: By default, ThinApp runtime will shutdown any services started within the virtual environment when the last non-service process is shutdown. You can disable this feature if you want to keep the services running.

  Example:

  ```
  [BuildOptions]
  AutoShutdownServices=0 (default=1)
  ```

- `AutoStartServices`: Normally, all virtualized services will start upon package launch. This may be quite time consuming, so you might want to consider disabling the auto-start of services.

  Example:

  ```
  [BuildOptions]
  AutoStartServices=0 (default=1)
  ```

- `BlockSize`: You can change the default block size used when compressing the package. The default block size is 64 KB. Valid block sizes are 128 KB, 256 KB, 512 KB, or 1 MB. You can change the block size for individual folders within your project by adding the `BlockSize` parameter to the folder's `##Attributes.ini` file.

  Example:

  ```
  [Compression]
  BlockSize=128k (k means KB and m means MB, e.g. 1m = 1MB)
  ```

- `CachePath`: `CachePath` is the location of the ThinApp package cache. The cache location is where virtualized fonts will be copied to in the physical environment prior to activation. This parameter can be overridden with the help of the `%THINSTALL_CACHE_DIR%` environment variable.

  Example:

  ```
  [BuildOptions]
  CachePath=C:\ThinAppCache (default is the user's local profile)
  ```

- `CapturedUsingVersion`: `CapturedUsingVersion` indicates which version of ThinApp is used to capture the application. You should not delete the parameter.

  Example:

  ```
  [BuildOptions]
  CapturedUsingVersion=4.7.1-677178
  ```

- `ChildProcessEnvironmentDefault`: By default, all child processes will be loaded within the virtual environment. Sometimes, this slows down the load process and you might want to consider loading child processes externally. Most of the time, you only want to load certain processes externally. In those cases, use the `ChildProcessEnvironmentExceptions` parameter instead.

  Example:

  ```
  [BuildOptions]
  ChildProcessEnvironmentDefault=External (default=virtual)
  ```

- ChildProcessEnvironmentExceptions:
  ChildProcessEnvironmentExceptions are used to add exceptions
  to the ChildProcessEnvironmentDefault parameter. Often, you leave
  ChildProcessEnvironmentDefault as the default, loading child processes
  virtually, and add the specific processes you want to load externally as
  ChildProcessEnvironmentExceptions. We separate processes by using
  a semicolon.

  Example:

  ```
  [BuildOptions]
  ChildProcessEnvironmentExceptions=WINWORD.EXE;EXCEL.EXE;POWERPNT.
  EXE;OUTLOOK.EXE;MOC.EXE
  ```

- CommandLine: CommandLine is used to add hardcoded parameters to your
  entry point's source executable.

  Example:

  ```
  [Entry Point Section]
  CommandLine="%ProgramFilesDir%\Mozilla Firefox\firefox.exe" -safe-
  mode
  ```

- Comment: Comment is specified per entry point, and determines what will be
  displayed when the user hovers the mouse over a shortcut to the entry point.
  If nothing is specified, the path to the entry point is displayed.

  Example:

  ```
  [Entry Point Section]
  Comment=This is your default browser
  ```

- CompressionType: The CompressionType parameter specifies if you
  want to compress the package or not. Back in the Thinstall days it was
  not only compression on and off, we were also offered **None**, **Fast** and
  Small compression. No one really used the Small algorithm so when
  VMware acquired Thinstall, they got rid of the Small option. By default,
  only files other than executables and dlls are compressed. You can
  change this behavior by using the OptimizedFor parameter. You can add
  CompressionType to a project folder's ##Attributes.ini file to compress
  only that folder.

  Example:

  ```
  [Compression]
  CompressionType=Fast (default=None)
  ```

- `DirectoryIsolationMode`: `DirectoryIsolationMode` specifies the default filesystem's isolation mode. The default isolation mode will be used if no isolation mode has been specified on a location. Valid parameters are **WriteCopy** or **Merged**. You should not use **Full** as your default directory isolation mode because you would probably hide too much of the native system from the package.

  Example:

  ```
  [Isolation]
  DirectoryIsolationMode=WriteCopy
  ```

- `DisableCutPaste`: Using this parameter will disable the ability to copy/cut and paste information out from the package.

  Example:

  ```
  [BuildOptions]
  DisableCutPaste=1 (default=0)
  ```

- `DisableCutPasteMsg`: This parameter specifies the text that will be pasted instead of the original data when using `DisableCutPaste=1`.

  Example:

  ```
  [BuildOptions]
  DisableCutPasteMsg=Administrator has disabled Cut and Paste for
  application %1s
  ```

- `Disabled`: This parameter is used to specify if an entry point should be created or not.

  Example:

  ```
  [Entry Point Section]
  Disabled=1 (0 will create the Entry Point)
  ```

- `DisablePrinting`: By using this parameter you can disable printing from a package. The end result, that the user can't print, is very similar to using the `HidePrinters` parameter.

  Example:

  ```
  [BuildOptions]
  DisablePrinting=1 (default=0)
  ```

- `DisableRegistryTransaction`: With ThinApp Version 4.5, the way the ThinApp runtime stores the virtual registry within the sandbox was changed. In Version 4.5, the registry is stored using a transactional log. This should make the sandbox more robust and less likely to become corrupted. The legacy method uses a flat file with a backup file containing the last known good version. At times you can have a performance issue when using the new format, especially when storing the sandbox on a network share. If this is the case, try using the legacy method instead. I don't recommend that you change this setting on all of your packages; it's something you should decide on a package-by-package basis.

  Example:

  ```
  [BuildOptions]
  DisableRegistryTransaction=1 (default=0)
  ```

- `DisableTracing`: This parameter will disable the possibility of using the Log Monitor to debug the execution of the package.

  Example:

  ```
  [BuildOptions]
  DisableTracing=1 (default 0)
  ```

- `ExcludePattern`: `ExcludePattern` will allow you to exclude certain files and folders from being compiled into the package. This way you can keep the installer cache within your project folder, but keep them from bloating your packages. Please note that `ExcludePattern` uses its own `Package.ini` section called `[FileList]`. You can add the parameter into `##Attributes.ini` files as well. This way, the exclusion will only be active on that specific folder.

  Example:

  ```
  [FileList]
  ExcludePattern=\.cab,\.msi
  ```

- `ExternalCOMObjects`: By default, ThinApp will keep virtualized COM objects virtual. If you suspect that an application implements COM objects that are incompatible with ThinApp runtime, you can have them load externally, outside of the virtualized environment. This is quite rare, and more or less only implemented when you have an issue and you're told by VMware support to use this feature. The parameter uses the CLSID keys.

  Example:

  ```
  [BuildOptions]
  ExternalCOMObjects={8BC3F05E-D86B-11D0-A075-
  00C04FB68820};{7D096C5F-AC08-4F1F-BEB7-5C22C517CE39}
  ```

- **ExternalDLLs**: Using the `ExternalDLLs` parameter, you can specify virtualized DLLs that should be loaded by the system rather than the ThinApp runtime. This is very handy if your application uses DLLs that ThinApp runtime doesn't support, for example, DLLs requiring hooking.

  Example:

  ```
  [BuildOptions]
  ExternalDLLs=one.dll;another.dll
  ```

- **FileTypes**: The `FileTypes` parameter will tell `thinreg.exe` what file type extensions to register to the entry point.

  Example:

  ```
  [Entry Point Section]
  FileTypes=.htm.html.shtml.xht.xhtml
  ```

- **ForcedVirtualLoadPaths**: The `ForcedVirtualLoadPaths` parameter tells ThinApp runtime to load physical DLLs within the virtual environment. This parameter is useful when an application must load external system DLLs that depend on DLL files located in the package.

  Example:

  ```
  [BuildOptions]
  ForcedVirtualLoadPaths=%ProgramFilesDir%\LocallyInstalledApp\
  LoadMe.dll
  ```

- **HidePrinters**: The `HidePrinters` parameter offers the same end result as the `DisablePrinting` parameter, that is, the end user can't print from the packaged application. `HidePrinters` will hide all printers for the virtualized application.

  Example:

  ```
  [BuildOptions]
  HidePrinters=1 (default=0)
  ```

- **Icon**: The `Icon` parameter will allow you to specify an icon for your entry point.

  Example:

  ```
  [Entry Point Section]
  Icon=%ProgramFilesDir%\Mozilla Firefox\MyOwnIcon.ico
  or
  Icon=%ProgramFilesDir%\Mozilla Firefox\firefox.exe,2 (Icon
  supports specifying specific icon within a file.)
  ```

- `IgnoreDDEMessages`: You can block DDE messages from getting passed into the virtualized application. By default, DDE messages are passed from the operating system into the virtual environment.

  Example:

  ```
  [BuildOptions]
  IgnoreDDEMessages=1 (default=0)
  ```

- `InventoryName`: Setup Capture picks up the value of `InventoryName` during the capturing process. Setup Capture investigates the `HKLM\SOFTWARE\Microsoft\Windows\CurrentVersion\Uninstall` and `HKCU\SOFTWARE\Microsoft\Windows\CurrentVersion\Uninstall` registry keys to learn the name of the application captured. If you capture multiple installers in one capture, you will probably have to modify the `InventoryName` parameter to reflect the true application name. `InventoryName` is used to prepopulate many `Package.ini` settings, such as `SandboxName`, `MSIFilename`, and many more. `InventoryName` is also used to populate the **Add or Remove Programs** window when registering the ThinApp package.

  Example:

  ```
  [BuildOptions]
  InventoryName=Mozilla Firefox (3.5.7)
  ```

- `InventoryIcon`: `InventoryIcon` is the application icon displayed on the Horizon Application Manager's workspace.

  Example:

  ```
  [BuildOptions]
  InventoryIcon=%ProgramFilesDir%\Mozilla Firefox\firefox.exe,0
  ```

- `IsolatedMemoryObjects`: The `IsolatedMemoryObjects` parameter can help when two applications, using the same shared memory object, conflict with each other. One example can be when you have one version of the application natively installed and another version virtualized.

  Example:

  ```
  [BuildOptions]
  IsolatedMemoryObjects=*outlook*;Some Other Object
  ```

- `IsolatedSynchronizationObjects`: The
  `IsolatedSynchronizationObjects` parameter allows you to isolate
  synchronization objects, for example: OpenMutex, CreateMutex,
  OpenSemaphore, CreateSemaphore, OpenEvent, and CreateEvent.
  If you have an issue and find any of these in the Log Monitor trace
  you might want to try isolating synchronization objects.

  Example:

  ```
  [BuildOptions]
  IsolatedSynchronizationObjects=*outlook*;Some Other Object
  ```

- `LoadDotNetFromSystem`: If your package includes .NET Framework, you
  can tell the package to discard the virtualized .NET and load the system .NET
  Framework on Windows 7 machines. This way, your package containing an
  older version of .NET can support both Windows XP and Windows 7.

  Example:

  ```
  [BuildOptions]
  LoadDotNetFromSystem=Win7
  ```

- `LocaleIdentifier`: `LocaleIdentifier` is a numeric ID identifying the
  language (locale) and will affect the layout and formatting of your virtualized
  application. By default, the locale of your capturing environment will be in
  your `Package.ini`.

  Example:

  ```
  [BuildOptions]
  LocaleIdentifier=1033
  ```

- `LocaleName`: The `LocaleName` parameter displays the name of the locale
  when you capture an application. This parameter is not added to `Package.
  ini` by default.

  Example:

  ```
  [BuildOptions]
  LocaleName=en-EN
  ```

- `LogPath`: The `LogPath` parameter specifies where the Log Monitor trace file
  will be created.

  Example:

  ```
  [BuildOptions]
  LogPath=C:\Temp
  ```

- `MetaDataContainerOnly`: The `MetaDataContainerOnly` parameter indicates that the entry point is only used as a data container.

  Example:

  ```
  [Entry Point Section]
  MetaDataContainerOnly=1
  ```

- `MSIArpProductIcon`: `MSIArpProductIcon` specifies the icon displayed in the **Add or Remove Programs** control panel window.

  Example:

  ```
  [BuildOptions]
  MSIArpProductIcon=%ProgramFilesDir%\Mozilla Firefox\firefox.exe,0
  ```

- `MSICompressionType`: You can decide to compress the MSI file content to preserve disk space. Supported values are **None** or **Fast**.

  Example:

  ```
  [BuildOptions]
  MSICompressionType=None
  ```

- `MSIDefaultInstallAllUsers`: This parameter specifies if the ThinApp generated MSI should be installed machine wide or per user.

  Example:

  ```
  [BuildOptions]
  MSIDefaultInstallAllUsers=0 (Default are 1, 2 will first try
  to install machine wide but if not able to revert to per user
  installation.)
  ```

- `MSIFilename`: When this is activated within your `Package.ini` file, the ThinApp build process will generate an MSI file to be used for deployment of the ThinApp package. The value of the parameter specifies the name of the file generated.

  Example:

  ```
  [BuildOptions]
  MSIFilename=Mozilla Firefox (3.5.7).msi
  ```

- `MSIInstallDirectory`: `MSIInstallDirectory` specifies the name of the folder where the ThinApp package will be deployed. By default, the name of the folder includes "(VMware ThinApp)". This is to make sure it won't conflict with any natively installed versions of the same application.

  Example:

  ```
  [BuildOptions]
  MSIInstallDirectory=Mozilla Firefox (3.5.7) (VMware ThinApp)
  ```

- `MSIManufacturer`: The `MSIManufacturer` will populate the manufacturer property in **Add or Remove Programs** when registering the package. The default value will be whatever company name you used when registering your capturing environment.

  Example:

  ```
  [BuildOptions]
  MSIManufacturer=Peter Björk
  ```

- `MSIProductCode`: Setup Capture will generate a unique **Globally Unique Identifier (GUID)** to identify the application deployed to your clients. Together with `MSIProductVersion`, it allows Windows installer to update already deployed packages with new versions. Normally, you should leave this parameter unmodified.

  Example:

  ```
  [BuildOptions]
  MSIProductCode={FA347819-9E28-3A88-BB20-46E3F1435C94}
  ```

- `MSIProductVersion`: `MSIProductVersion` is used to identify a new version of the package. If you raise the number, the build process will automatically create an update package capable of uninstalling previous versions of the package and deploy the new version automatically.

  Example:

  ```
  [BuildOptions]
  MSIProductVersion=2.0 (default=1.0)
  ```

- `MSIProperty.`: With `MSIProperty.` you can add your own properties to the MSI file generated by ThinApp.

  Example:

  ```
  [BuildOptions]
  MSIProperty.MyCustomProperty=AnyValueYouWant
  ```

- `MSIRequireElevatedPrivileges`: `MSIRequireElevatedPrivileges` specifies whether installing the MSI file requires elevated privileges or not. If required, the user will get a UAC prompt on Vista or newer operating systems. Installing per user only should not require elevated privileges.

  Example:

  ```
  [BuildOptions]
  MSIRequireElevatedPrivileges=0 (default=1)
  ```

- `MSIStreaming`: This parameter was called `MSIUseCabs` in previous versions of ThinApp. `MSIStreaming` tells the build process if it should include the package in the MSI file it generates or keep the package files outside. When the package files are stored within the MSI file, the filesystem is virtualized within the MSI file. This makes it impossible to use MSI editing tools like Orca to change the MSI file. If you keep the package files outside the MSI file (`MSIStreaming=1`), it will be possible to modify the MSI file using a traditional MSI editing tool. When using VMware View Manager to entitle ThinApp packages, `MSIStreaming=1` will allow for a streaming deployment.

  Example:

  ```
  [BuildOptions]
  MSIStreaming=1 (default=0)
  ```

- `MSIUpgradeCode`: The `MSIUpgradeCode` parameter works together with the `MSIProductVersion` and the `MSIProductCode` parameters to identify if an MSI package is an update to an existing deployment. You can often leave this parameter unmodified, only changing the `MSIProductVersion` parameter, and the build process will automatically generate an update MSI file.

  Example:

  ```
  [BuildOptions]
  MSIUpgradeCode={8A07FD29-1500-3A60-27AD-C761175F7F79}
  ```

- `NetRelaunch`: `NetRelaunch` was introduced as a workaround to Symantec Antivirus interfering with the streaming of ThinApp packages. Nowadays, `NetRelaunch` is activated by default. When active, the package will relaunch itself upon streaming. This way, only a small part of the package will be accessed and therefore scanned by your antivirus initially. I know no real reason for changing this parameter. Just leave it as default. What you should do is to make sure to disable on-access antivirus scanning of your ThinApp repository.

  Example:

  ```
  [BuildOptions]
  NetRelaunch=1 (this is the default value)
  ```

- NotificationDLLs: When using the NotificationDLLs parameter, the ThinApp runtime will call a third-party DLL to provide notification of events, for example, startup and shutdown. This parameter is used when using Horizon Application Manager for entitlement.

  Example:

  ```
  [BuildOptions]
  NotificationDLLs=HorizonPlugin.dll
  ```

- NotificationDLLSignatures: The NotificationDLLSignatures parameter works hand-in-hand with the NotificationDLLs parameter to verify the signature of the DLL. If the DLL lacks the signature, ThinApp runtime will not load the file.

  Example:

  ```
  [BuildOptions]
  NotificationDLLSignatures=VMware, Inc.
  ```

- ObjectTypes: ObjectTypes will specify which COM object types thinreg.exe will register on the local operating system when registering a package. Setup Capture will pick up any object types registered during your capturing process and add the information to your entry point section.

  Example:

  ```
  [Entry Point Section]
  ObjectTypes=Word.Application;Word.Application.12;Word.
  Application.8;Word.Backup.8;Word.Basic;Word.Basic.8;Word.
  Basic.9;Word.Document;Word.Document.12;Word.Document.8;Word.
  DocumentMacroEnabled;Word.DocumentMacroEnabled.12;Word.
  Picture;Word.Picture.8;Word.RTF.8;Word.Template;Word.
  Template.12;Word.Template.8;Word.TemplateMacroEnabled;Word.
  TemplateMacroEnabled.12;Word.Wizard.8
  ```

- OptimizedFor: This parameter goes hand-in-hand with the CompressionType parameter. Using OptimizedFor, you can change from the default behavior of only compressing files other than executables and dlls. OptimizedFor=Disk will compress all files. The downside of compressing all files is decreased performance. The package will launch slower if all files are compressed. Compressing all files will also disable the ThinApp runtime's memory sharing functionality.

  Example:

  ```
  [Compression]
  OptimizedFor=Disk (default=Memory)
  ```

- `OptionalAppLinks`: `OptionalAppLinks` will activate AppLink functionality in your package. `OptionalAppLinks` will integrate to the child packages found but will allow for package launch if no AppLinks can be found.

  Example:

  ```
  [BuildOptions]
  OptionalAppLinks=C:\Program Files\Java Runtime\java.exe
  ```

- `OutDir`: The `OutDir` parameter specifies where the output from the build process will be stored.

  Example:

  ```
  [BuildOptions]
  OutDir=bin
  ```

- `PermittedComputersSIDs`: `PermittedComputersSIDs` specifies which computer SIDs are allowed to execute the package. It works similar to `PermittedGroups`, but is computer-based rather than user-based.

- `PermittedComputersAccessDeniedMsg`: This parameter specifies the message displayed to the end user if their computer isn't allowed to launch the ThinApp package.

  Example:

  ```
  [BuildOptions]
  PermittedComputersAccessDeniedMsg=Your machine is not entitled to
  run this application.
  ```

- `PermittedGroups`: `PermittedGroups` is used to protect your packages. Only a user, who is a member of the Active Directory groups specified with `PermittedGroups`, will be able to use the package. The parameter supports adding the group's SID instead of group name. `PermittedGroups` can be applied package wide and/or per entry point.

  Example:

  ```
  [BuildOptions]
  PermittedGroups=ThinApp Users
  or
  [Entry Point Section]
  PermittedGroups=Mozilla Firefox Users
  ```

- PermittedGroupSIDs: `PermittedGroupSIDs` can be used to specify an Active Directory group's SID for protecting a package.

  Example:

  ```
  [BuildOptions]
  PermittedGroupSIDs=Enter the group's SID
  ```

- PreventDllInjection: `PreventDllInjection` prevents a DLL from being loaded into a process when another process is calling `SetWindowHook` to set a global hook using the DLL.

  Example:

  ```
  [BuildOptions]
  PreventDllInjection=1 (default=0)
  ```

- ProcessExternalNameBehavior: By default, the original process name is hidden by the ThinApp runtime. This will allow most whitelist security products to work with ThinApp packages. The reason is that the name in the process list is the same as the filename on disk. You can change this using the `ProcessExternalNameBehavior` parameter.

  Example:

  ```
  [BuildOptions]
  ProcessExternalNameBehavior=Original (default=WhitelistFriendly)
  ```

- Protocols: `Protocols` specifies which protocols will be registered to an entry point. Setup Capture will pick up the protocols registered during the capturing process.

  Example:

  ```
  [Entry Point Section]
  Protocols=FirefoxURL;ftp;http;https
  ```

- QualityReportingEnabled: The `QualityReportingEnabled` parameter specifies whether the package will deliver anonymous data to VMware or not. `QualityReportingEnabled=1` will send data to VMware.

  Example:

  ```
  [BuildOptions]
  QualityReportingEnabled=0 (The package will not deliver any data
  to VMware)
  ```

- `QualityReportingTag`: The anonymous data passed to VMware using `QualityReportingEnabled=1` can be tagged to identify the origin of the package. This is done using the `QualityReportingTag` parameter, and to my knowledge it's only used within the ThinApp Factory. More information about ThinApp Factory can be found here: `http://labs.vmware.com/flings/thinapp-factory`.

  Example:

  ```
  [BuildOptions]
  QualityReportingTag="ThinAppFactory"
  ```

- `ReadOnlyData`: This parameter specifies the file that is the data container. There can only be one data container per package.

  Example:

  ```
  [Entry Point Section]
  ReadOnlyData=Package.ro.tvr
  ```

- `RegistryIsolationMode`: The default registry isolation mode is always WriteCopy. Using the `RegistryIsolationMode` parameter allows you to change the default isolation mode.

  Example:

  ```
  [BuildOptions]
  RegistryIsolationMode=Merged (default=WriteCopy)
  ```

- `RemoveSandboxOnExit`: This parameter allows you to wipe the sandbox clean on every exit of the package.

  Example:

  ```
  [BuildOptions]
  RemoveSandboxOnExit=1 (default=0)
  ```

- `RemoveSandboxOnStart`: `RemoveSandboxOnStart` is a new parameter. Like its sister parameter; `RemoveSandboxOnExit`, it will delete the sandbox content. `RemoveSandboxOnStart` will delete the sandbox on each start of the Package. This can be handy if you want to make sure the sandbox is always cleared. Using only the `RemoveSandboxOnExit` parameter might not be enough. If the packaged application crashes, `RemoveSandboxOnExit` will not receive a correct exit code from the application and will therefore not delete the sandbox.

  Example:

  ```
  [BuildOptions]
  RemoveSandboxOnStart=1 (default=0)
  ```

- RequiredAppLinks: RequiredAppLinks will activate AppLink functionality in your package. RequiredAppLinks will deny package launch if it cannot access the AppLink package.

  Example:

  ```
  [BuildOptions]
  RequiredAppLinks=C:\Program Files\Oracle Client\OracleClient.exe
  ```

- ReserveExtraAddressSpace: The ReserveExtraAddressSpace parameter specifies the amount of extra address space to reserve for the captured executable file.

  Example:

  ```
  [Entry Point Section]
  ReserveExtraAddressSpace=512K
  ```

- RetainAllIcons: To save disk space, ThinApp removes unused icons from the package. You can decide to keep the icons if needed.

  Example:

  ```
  [Entry Point Section]
  RetainAllIcons=1 (default=0)
  ```

- RuntimeEULA: RuntimeEULA is probably the least used Package.ini parameter you will find. Activating RuntimeEULA will display the VMware ThinApp EULA when launching the package. VMware doesn't require that you display the EULA so I honestly do not see any point in ever activating the parameter.

  Example:

  ```
  [BuildOptions]
  RuntimeEULA=1 (default=0)
  ```

- SandboxCOMObjects: You can modify the SandboxCOMObjects parameter to make COM objects, registered within the virtual environment, visible outside the virtual environment. By default, virtual COM objects are not visible in the physical environment.

  Example:

  ```
  [BuildOptions]
  SandboxCOMObjects=1 (default=0)
  ```

- SandboxName: The SandboxName parameter specifies the name of the sandbox.

  Example:

  ```
  [BuildOptions]
  SandboxName=Mozilla Firefox
  ```

- SandboxNetworkDrives: By default, network drives are not sandboxed. You can activate sandboxing of network drives using SandboxNetworkDrives=1.

  Example:

  ```
  [BuildOptions]
  SandboxNetworkDrives=1 (default=0)
  ```

- SandboxPath: This parameter specifies the location of the sandbox.

  Example:

  ```
  [BuildOptions]
  SandboxPath=C:\Sandboxes
  ```

- SandboxRemovableDisk: Removable disks are not sandboxed by default. This parameter allows you to change this behavior.

  Example:

  ```
  [BuildOptions]
  SandboxRemovableDisk=1 (default=0)
  ```

- Services: ThinApp allows virtualized services to be registered, and thereby starts during the boot of the operating system, on the native system. The service still lives within the virtual environment. To be able to register a service natively, you need to activate the service as an entry point and activate the service parameter. The value of the Services parameter is the name of the service. Setup Capture will grab information on any services registered during the capturing process and prepopulate your Package.ini file with the correct values. The service entry point is disabled by default. You must register machine wide in order for the service to be registered correctly. This means using thinreg.exe with the /a switch.

  Example:

  ```
  [Entry Point Section]
  Services=Apache2.2
  ```

- `SetVirtualModuleFileNameInPeb`: `SetVirtualModuleFileNameInPeb=0` (default) sets the entry point file path in **Process Environment Block (PEB)**, and applies it to all virtual child processes. When using `SetVirtualModuleFileNameInPeb=1` (default value in ThinApp Version 4.5 – 4.6), PEB contains the virtual EXE's file path, which doesn't exist on the physical operating system. This means Windows Explorer can't always find the correct icon to use. You should very rarely have to use this parameter.

  Example:

  ```
  [BuildOptions]
  SetVirtualModuleFileNameInPeb=0
  ```

- `Shortcut`: The `Shortcut` parameter tells the entry point in which file the data container is stored.

  Example:

  ```
  [Entry Point Section]
  Shortcut=Mozilla Firefox.exe
  ```

- `Shortcuts`: The `Shortcuts` parameter is used when registering a package, and specifies where shortcuts will be created.

  Example:

  ```
  [Entry Point Section]
  Shortcuts=%Desktop%;%Programs%\Mozilla Firefox
  ```

- `Source`: The `Source` parameter identifies the target of the entry point, that is, what will be launched within the virtual environment. The source can be located either within or outside the virtual environment. The source does not have to be an executable as long as the file type extension is registered to an application.

  Example:

  ```
  [Entry Point Section]
  Source=%ProgramFilesDir%\Mozilla Firefox\firefox.exe
  ```

- `StatusbarDisplayName`: With the help of the `StatusbarDisplayName` parameter you can change the application name displayed in the ThinApp splash screen.

  Example:

  ```
  [BuildOptions]
  StatusbarDisplayName=Mozilla Firefox
  ```

- `StripVersionInfo`: By default, the ThinApp package will keep the entry point target's version information and add them to the entry point. You can strip the version information using the `StripVersionInfo` parameter.

  Example:

  ```
  [Entry Point Section]
  StripVersionInfo=1 (default=0)
  ```

- `ThinDirectWhitelistOnly`: The `ThinDirectWhitelistOnly` parameter allows you to specify whether or not a browser package should redirect back to the default browser. The default behavior is to redirect the user to the default browser if visiting any URL not ThinDirected to the package.

  Example:

  ```
  [BuildOptions]
  ThinDirectWhitelistOnly=0 (default=1)
  ```

- `UACRequestedPrivilegesLevel`: You can modify the `UACRequestedPrivilegesLevel` parameter to specify which privileges your package requires on an operating system supporting **User Account Control (UAC)**. Possible values are: `asInvoker` (default), `requireAdministrator`, or `highestAvailable`. `highestAvailable` will use the highest privilege possible avoiding UAC prompt.

  Example:

  ```
  [BuildOptions]
  UACRequestedPrivilegesLevel=highestAvailable
  ```

- `UACRequestedPrivilegesUiAccess`: This parameter specifies access or no access to protected user interface elements. Possible values are `false` or `true`.

  Example:

  ```
  [BuildOptions]
  UACRequestedPrivilegesUiAccess=false (no access to protected
  elements)
  ```

- `UpgradePath`: `UpgradePath` is an interesting parameter. When using in-place update it will be used to specify where the package searches for updated versions of itself. If your package uses AppSync, `UpgradePath` will be the location where the AppSync cache, log, and update package is stored.

  Example:

  ```
  [BuildOptions]
  UpgradePath=C:\Updates
  ```

- Version.: The Version. parameter populates the version tab of the entry point's file properties with custom information.

  Example:

  ```
  [Entry Point Section]
  Version.AnythingYouWant=VeryImportantValue
  ```

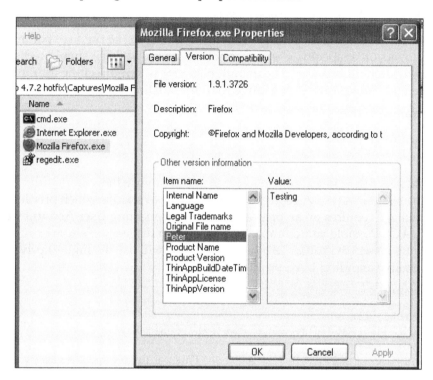

You can add your own file version properties. The Package.ini settings of the previous picture are as follows:

```
[Mozilla Firefox.exe]
Source=%ProgramFilesDir%\Mozilla Firefox\firefox.exe
ReadOnlyData=Package.ro.tvr
Version.Peter=Testing
```

- `VirtualComputerName`: ThinApp can virtualize the hostname. This is handy when the packaged application refers to the hostname where it was originally installed. Virtualizing the hostname can help in making the package portable. Another workaround may be to capture the application on a machine using `LOCALHOST` as the hostname. The default behavior is to pass the native hostname to the virtualized application.

  Example:

  ```
  [BuildOptions]
  VirtualComputerName=MACHINE1
  ```

- `VirtualDrives`: ThinApp can virtualize drives. By default, the C-drive of your capturing environment is virtualized. This way, the serial number of the C-drive is virtualized. This helps in making some legacy applications portable. `VirtualDrives` uses a couple of parameters to define the virtual drive it creates. `Drive=` specifies the drive letter of the virtual drive. `Serial=` specifies the serial number of the virtual drive. `Serial=` is not required. `Type=` specifies what kind of drive ThinApp will pretend that the virtual drive is. Possible values are `REMOVABLE`, `RAMDISK`, `CDROM`, and `FIXED`. Your package can only have one `VirtualDrives` parameter active. You separate each virtual drive with a semicolon.

  Example:

  ```
  [BuildOptions]
  VirtualDrives=Drive=a, Serial=00de1968, Type=REMOVABLE; Drive=c,
  Serial=647c820d, Type=FIXED; Drive=d, Serial=647c820d, Type=CDROM
  ```

- `VirtualElevation`: `VirtualElevation=1` means the ThinApp runtime will lie to the app and tell it that it's running as an elevated process. `VirtualElevation=0` means ThinApp runtime will pass the true elevation status to the application. So this is a bit different from `UACRequestedPrivilegesLevel`, which really affects the elevation status. `VirtualElevation` only affects what ThinApp runtime will tell the process.

  Example:

  ```
  [BuildOptions]
  VirtualElevation=1
  ```

- VirtualizeExternalOutOfProcessCOM:
  VirtualizeExternalOutOfProcessCOM specifies if ThinApp will run an external process, called by using COM, within the virtual environment or not. By default, such a process is run within the virtualized environment.

  Example:

  ```
  [BuildOptions]
  VirtualizeExternalOutOfProcessCOM=0 (default=1)
  ```

- WorkingDirectory: The WorkingDirectory parameter specifies what will be the working directory for the application launched. If not specified, the working directory will be the location of the package.

  Example:

  ```
  [Entry Point Section]
  WorkingDirectory=%ProgramFilesDir%\Mozilla Firefox
  ```

- Wow64: The Wow64 parameter tries to simulate a 32-bit environment when the package is running on a 64-bit operating system. If your 32-bit application has a problem running on a 64-bit system you can try to activate this parameter. It will only help a few applications but is still worth trying.

  Example:

  ```
  [BuildOptions]
  Wow64=0
  ```

- XYZ=AnyValue: You can add anything to Package.ini and it will be accessible via vb-scripting or the ThinApp SDK. This way, you can pick up custom settings with your script.

  Example:

  ```
  [BuildOptions]
  MyNameIs=Peter_Bjork
  ```

There are a couple of Package.ini parameters related to VMware Horizon Application Manager. You'll find them in your Package.ini under the Horizon Parameters headline.

- AppID=genid: AppID is a unique application identifier used by Horizon to be able to track and manage the package.

- NotificationDLLs=HorizonPlugin.dll: The NotificationDLLs parameter tells the ThinApp runtime that it has to ask the HorizonPlugin.dll for entitlement before allowing execution of the package.

- `HorizonOrgUrl=http://www.MyHorizonXYZ.com`: The `HorizonOrgUrl` value should point to your Horizon Workspace URL. When specified, the end user will be presented with a link to download the Horizon Agent, if it's not already installed on the same machine that the ThinApp package is executed on.

- `VersionID=`: `VersionID` is used by Horizon to identify updated versions of already managed packages.

Environment variables and ThinApp runtime switches

- **THINSTALL_BIN**: It specifies the location of the ThinApp utilities folder. You can find out more information about the **THINSTALL_BIN** environment variable in *Chapter 1*, *Application Virtualization*.

- **%TS_NO_FONTS%**: Specifying the `%TS_NO_FONTS%` environment variable will disable virtualized fonts. The environment variable's value is of no importance. Having a lot of virtualized fonts might slow down the performance of your package. Specifying `%TS_NO_FONTS%` allows you to launch the package with no fonts. This way, you can easily compare performance with or without fonts included in the package.

Changing the sandbox location

With the help of an environment variable, you can override the sandbox location. Supported environment variables are `%THINSTALL_SANDBOX_DIR%` and `%SandboxName_SANDBOX_DIR%`. These environment variables are discussed more in depth in the *The sandbox* section in *Chapter 1*, *Application Virtualization*.

- **%THINSTALL_CACHE_DIR%**: You use this environment variable to override the `CachePath Package.ini` parameter. For more information about the `CachePath`, please see the *Package.ini parameters* section in this appendix.

- **%TS_OPTIONS%**: `%TS_OPTIONS%` is created automatically by ThinApp runtime and only exists in the virtual environment. It points to the entry point.

- **%TS_ORIGIN%**: `%TS_ORIGIN%` environment variable only exists within the virtual environment. `%TS_ORIGIN%` points to the package's data container.

ThinApp runtime switches

There is to my knowledge only one switch that the ThinApp runtime will listen to, and that is **-ThinstallVersion**. The **ThinstallVersion** switch will show you which ThinApp runtime version the package contains. All other switches added to a package will be passed through to the virtualized executable (the source of the entry point).

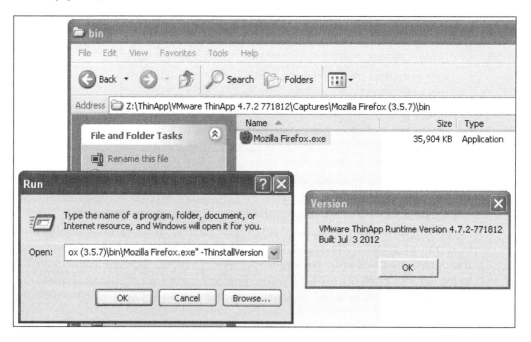

Summary

In this appendix, I have covered the `Package.ini` supported folder macros, environment variables, and ThinApp runtime switches. This appendix can be used as a reference for all possible `Package.ini` setting.

This concludes the book on ThinApp 4.7 Essentials. I hope you found the book useful and that it will help you with your daily ThinApp packaging.

If you are looking for more ThinApp information, can I recommend the official VMware ThinApp blog, `http://blogs.vmware.com/thinapp`. Since it's a blog, articles will be archived per month published and you will have to search to find what you are looking for. There are some categories you can sort on, but not all articles are created with a category. Personally, I use `http://google.com` to search the blog. I've found Google to be much more precise in its search result than the blog's own search engine.

The ThinApp community, `http://communities.vmware.com/community/vmtn/desktop/thinapp`, is another great resource for information.

Index

Thank you for buying
VMware ThinApp 4.7 Essentials

About Packt Publishing

Packt, pronounced 'packed', published its first book "Mastering phpMyAdmin for Effective MySQL Management" in April 2004 and subsequently continued to specialize in publishing highly focused books on specific technologies and solutions.

Our books and publications share the experiences of your fellow IT professionals in adapting and customizing today's systems, applications, and frameworks. Our solution based books give you the knowledge and power to customize the software and technologies you're using to get the job done. Packt books are more specific and less general than the IT books you have seen in the past. Our unique business model allows us to bring you more focused information, giving you more of what you need to know, and less of what you don't.

Packt is a modern, yet unique publishing company, which focuses on producing quality, cutting-edge books for communities of developers, administrators, and newbies alike. For more information, please visit our website: www.packtpub.com.

About Packt Enterprise

In 2010, Packt launched two new brands, Packt Enterprise and Packt Open Source, in order to continue its focus on specialization. This book is part of the Packt Enterprise brand, home to books published on enterprise software – software created by major vendors, including (but not limited to) IBM, Microsoft and Oracle, often for use in other corporations. Its titles will offer information relevant to a range of users of this software, including administrators, developers, architects, and end users.

Writing for Packt

We welcome all inquiries from people who are interested in authoring. Book proposals should be sent to author@packtpub.com. If your book idea is still at an early stage and you would like to discuss it first before writing a formal book proposal, contact us; one of our commissioning editors will get in touch with you.

We're not just looking for published authors; if you have strong technical skills but no writing experience, our experienced editors can help you develop a writing career, or simply get some additional reward for your expertise.

VMware View 5 Desktop Virtualization Solutions

ISBN: 978-1-84968-112-4   Paperback: 288 pages

A complete guide to planning and designing solutions based on VMware View 5

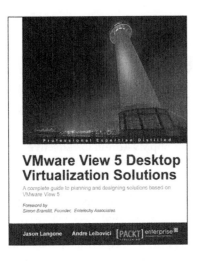

1. Written by VMware experts Jason Langone and Andre Leibovici, this book is a complete guide to planning and designing a solution based on VMware View 5

2. Secure your Visual Desktop Infrastructure (VDI) by having firewalls, antivirus, virtual enclaves, USB redirection and filtering and smart card authentication

3. Work with the JRockit Mission Control 3.1/4.0 tools suite to debug or profile your Java applications

Citrix XenServer 6.0 Administration Essential Guide

ISBN: 978-1-84968-616-7   Paperback: 364 pages

Deploy and manage XenServer in your enterprise to create, integrate, manage, and automate a virtual datacenter quickly and easily

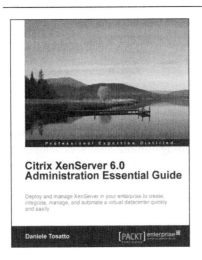

1. This book and eBook will take you through deploying XenServer in your enterprise, and teach you how to create and maintain your datacenter.

2. Manage XenServer and virtual machines using Citrix management tools and the command line.

3. Organize secure access to your infrastructure using role-based access control.

Please check **www.PacktPub.com** for information on our titles

**Getting Started with
Citrix XenApp 6.5**

Design and implement Citrix farms based on XenApp 6.5

Guillermo Musumeci

[PACKT] enterprise

Getting Started with Citrix XenApp 6.5

ISBN: 978-1-84968-666-2   Paperback: 478 pages

Design and implement Citrix farms based on XenApp 6.5

1. Use Citrix management tools to publish applications and resources on client devices with this book and eBook

2. Deploy and optimize XenApp 6.5 on Citrix XenServer, VMware ESX, and Microsoft Hyper-V virtual machines and physical servers

3. Understand new features included in XenApp 6.5 including a brand new chapter on advanced XenApp deployment covering topics such as unattended install of XenApp 6.5, using dynamic data center provisioning, and more

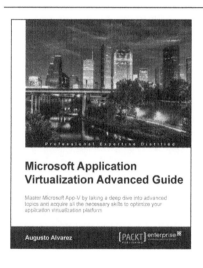

**Microsoft Application
Virtualization Advanced Guide**

Master Microsoft App-V by taking a deep dive into advanced topics and acquire all the necessary skills to optimize your application virtualization platform

Augusto Alvarez

[PACKT] enterprise

Microsoft Application Virtualization Advanced Guide

ISBN: 978-1-84968-448-4   Paperback: 474 pages

Master Microsoft App-V by taking a deep dive into advanced topics and acquire all the necessary skills to optimize your application virtualization platform

1. Understand advanced topics in App-V; identify some rarely known components and options available in the platform

2. Acquire advanced guidelines on how to troubleshoot App-V installations, sequencing, and application deployments

3. Learn how to handle particular applications, adapting companys' policies to the implementation, enforcing application licenses, securing the environment, and so on

Please check **www.PacktPub.com** for information on our titles

CPSIA information can be obtained at www.ICGtesting.com
Printed in the USA
LVOW03s1148141213

365316LV00008B/719/P